IMAGES (

MW00605209

CHINA AND JAPAN
AT WAR
1937–1945

This stylized illustration from the cover of a French magazine published in October 1937 depicts a resolute Nationalist Chinese soldier looking into the distance. The caption says that this is a 'typical Chinese soldier fighting against the Japanese in defence of Shanghai'. World opinion was generally on the side of the Chinese in 1937 as they were seen as victims of Japanese aggression.

IMAGES OF WAR

CHINA AND JAPAN AT WAR 1937–1945

RARE PHOTOGRAPHS FROM WARTIME ARCHIVES

Philip S. Jowett

Pen & Sword
MILITARY

First published in Great Britain in 2016 by
PEN & SWORD MILITARY
an imprint of
Pen & Sword Books Ltd,
47 Church Street,
Barnsley,
South Yorkshire
S70 2AS

A CIP record for this book is available from the British Library.

ISBN 978 1 47382 752 3

Typeset by CHIC GRAPHICS

Printed and bound by CPI Group (UK) Ltd, Croydon, CR0 4YY

Pen & Sword Books Ltd incorporates the imprints of Pen & Sword Archaeology,
Atlas, Aviation, Battleground, Discovery, Family History, History, Maritime, Military,
Naval, Politics, Railways, Select, Social History, Transport, True Crime, Claymore
Press, Frontline Books, Leo Cooper, Praetorian Press, Remember When, Seaforth
Publishing and Wharncliffe.

For a complete list of Pen & Sword titles please contact
Pen & Sword Books Limited
47 Church Street, Barnsley, South Yorkshire, S70 2AS, England
E-mail: enquiries@pen-and-sword.co.uk
Website: www.pen-and-sword.co.uk

Contents

Dedication

This book is dedicated to my much-loved sister Stephanie

Preface

The Sino-Japanese War began in July 1937 and was one of the most destructive conflicts of the twentieth century. It resulted in the deaths of millions of Chinese soldiers and civilians and hundreds of thousands of Japanese servicemen. What began as yet another local armed incident between Chinese and Japanese units in northern China soon escalated into full-scale war. The Japanese empire and China had been unofficially at war since 1931 and there had been a series of short-lived and often small-scale conflicts in 1931, 1932, 1933 and 1936. These wars were born out of Japanese territorial aggression in Manchuria and northern China, and this went largely unchallenged by the Chinese Nationalist government. Japanese aggression was not always coordinated and local Imperial army commanders were often beyond the control of the weak civilian government in Tokyo. Whatever the intention of the Japanese military, its savage war against China was to cause untold suffering for its people. Japan treated China as a subject nation and its people as slaves to be exploited for the greater glory of the emperor and the Japanese empire. The Chinese people's resistance to the Japanese was seen as an affront to the invaders and was met with brutality on a scale rarely seen in modern conflicts. Its long-term consequences would affect not only the fate of the Chinese nation but also the relationship between these two great Asian nations to this day.

The intention of this book is to provide the general student of military history with a well-illustrated guide to the Sino-Japanese War. The photographs included here tell the story of the eight-year war and its consequences for the Chinese nation. Starting with the invasion of China by the Japanese Imperial Armed Forces in July 1937, the book concludes with the final defeat of Japan in the Second World War in August 1945. All the combatants who participated in this multi-sided war with the Japanese are featured – Chinese Nationalist, Communist and Collaborationist forces. The war was complicated with civil war between the Chinese Nationalists and Communists often hampering the anti-Japanese war effort. After 7 December 1941 the war was swallowed up by the greater conflict between the Japanese empire and the Allied powers. China, along with neighbouring Burma, became another theatre of the all-encompassing world conflict. Alongside the world war, the various Chinese factions continued their own bitter struggle for the future of China after August 1945.

Acknowledgements

I would like to thank anyone who has assisted me over the years with information and photographs for my publications. For this book I would like to thank John Cloake, Gavin Goh, Ted Nevill at Cody Images, Mariusz Zimny and Wawrzyniec Markowski.

All the photographs apart from those listed below are from the Philip Jowett collection.

John Cloake: p. 122 (top)
Cody Images: pp. 96 (top) and 114 (top)
Gavin Goh: p. 85 (top)
Wawrzyniec Markowski: pp. 48 (top), 80 and 97 (bottom)
Mariusz Zimny: p. 60 (top)

Introduction

The late nineteenth and early twentieth centuries saw a major shift in the power balance in East Asia as a new military power emerged. Up until the mid-nineteenth century East Asia had been dominated for centuries by the Chinese Qing empire. Although China had suffered periods of decline over the years, no regional power existed that could challenge the Qing empire's supremacy. This all changed in the mid-nineteenth century when the historically isolated Japanese empire reluctantly began to open up its ports to Western traders. Many traditionalists in Japan were hostile to this trade and the resultant Western influence over the empire. Regardless of the complaints of traditionalists, a period of unprecedented modernization took place over just a few decades which created, at least on the surface, a forward-looking nation. Over the next forty years Japan rapidly developed from a traditional, almost medieval nation to a modern, ambitious state with an up-to-date army and navy. Some of the old military class chose to ignore this process, while others realized that this was the only way to stop European exploitation. The Meiji emperor actively encouraged his army to import the latest rifles, artillery and ships so that it could defend itself against any European military aggression. He saw what had happened to Imperial China following their defeat in the Opium Wars (1839–60). After China opened its ports to Western traders military force was used to compel the Chinese to buy Western goods, including opium.

This new Japan soon began to look to expand its influence onto mainland Asia and by 1894 was ready to challenge the ramshackle Chinese empire militarily. That year a dispute over control of supposedly independent Korea led to a full-scale war between the two powers, known as the First Sino-Japanese War (1894–5). Fought both in Korea and Manchuria, on land and at sea, the war was a disaster for the Chinese and ended with Japan's complete victory. This left China open to further foreign exploitation as the European powers demanded trade concessions from the Qing emperor. A deeply humiliated Chinese empire was now forced to consider modernizing in preparation for inevitable further clashes with Japan.

Over the next sixteen years the empire faced further ignominy following the Boxer Rebellion of 1900 and the Russo-Japanese War of 1904–5. The latter conflict saw China and its Manchurian provinces used as a battleground by the combatants.

At the end of the war victorious Japan was now the undisputed power in Asia and, having taken over Russia's territorial concessions in Manchuria, was now prone to dominating China. In 1911 the corrupt and inept Qing dynasty was finally overthrown and the emperor was replaced by a Chinese Republic which soon descended into chaos. The next seventeen years in Chinese history is known as the 'warlord era' when local military governors, or 'warlords', fought each other. The warlords ignored a series of weak civil governments in Peking and pursued their own power struggle, forming and breaking alliances throughout the 1910s and 1920s. Some warlords accepted Japanese military assistance as the latter hoped to exercise influence over whatever military group came to dominate China.

In the early 1920s a nationalist revolutionary party, the Kuomintang, began a campaign to reunite China under one government. Formed by a long-term revolutionary, Sun Yat-sen, the Kuomintang was taken over on his death in 1925 by the party's military leader, Chiang Kai-shek. Chiang and his National Revolutionary Army (NRA) triumphed in a two-year crusade known as the Northern Expedition. By 1928 the Northern Expedition had succeeded in defeating all of the warlords, either in battle or by negotiation. Chiang and his NRA had finally beaten their enemies and formed a Nationalist government, with its new capital in the city of Nanking. Their victory was short-lived as Chiang's leadership was never fully accepted by his rivals within the Nationalist camp. Fighting between these various factions in 1929 and 1930 ended again with victory for Chiang Kai-shek in the so-called 'Great Plains War'. Again, Chiang's success did not endure as the Japanese had been preparing to challenge the new Nationalist government of China. Japanese troops stationed in northern China had already clashed with NRA troops in 1928. For the first time Chiang had backed down when faced by Japanese garrisons that would not be moved from the concessions that had been granted to them in 1900.

In 1931 the Japanese finally struck when their troops stationed in parts of the three Chinese provinces of Manchuria staged an 'incident'. The 'Mukden Incident' saw fighting between Japanese and Chinese units in southern Manchuria in September 1931. The Japanese took over the city of Mukden and then gained ground into the rest of Manchuria, facing little resistance. Chiang Kai-shek had instructed his commanders in Manchuria to withdraw in front of the Japanese advance. This was in order that the world would see the Japanese as the aggressor and China as the victim. International outrage at Japan's actions did not worry them, however, and by mid-1932 they had taken most of Manchuria, setting up a client state called Manchukuo. A well-organized Chinese boycott of Japanese goods in retaliation for their invasion of Manchuria badly hurt the Japanese economy. When some Japanese residents in Shanghai, the main trading city in China, were attacked by Chinese rioters the Japanese military struck again. Japanese marines were landed in the city in late January 1932 and fighting with the local Chinese troops continued until May. The fighting ended with a peace treaty but before long Japan's territorial ambitions were to result in further conflict.

In 1933 the Japanese took over the Chinese province of Jehol, which bordered their newly conquered client state Manchukuo. Japan was not worried by the disapproval of the League of Nations and they began their invasion of Jehol in late February 1933. The action was followed on 27 March by their withdrawal from the League of Nations. Japan had simply claimed that Jehol was historically part of Manchuria and therefore should be included in the territory of Manchukuo. Resistance to the Japanese invasion was poorly organized and the ease of their victory led the Imperial army to plan further acts of aggression. The Japanese moved troops southwards into northern China and although the Chinese fought hard, the Japanese advanced to the gates of Peking. Again, a peace treaty was signed in May 1933 with the Japanese demanding the demilitarization of Chinese territory south of the Great Wall. They insisted that the Great Wall should form the boundary between Manchukuo and northern China and the demilitarized zone would avoid further clashes. Once more the Chinese had to concede territory and other rights to the Japanese, who threatened more aggression unless Chiang Kai-shek's government agreed to their terms. Chiang Kai-shek was obsessed with his campaign to defeat his Chinese Communist enemies and saw the loss of some territory in far-off northern China as temporary.

Over the next few years the Japanese and their secret service made further incursions, both militarily and politically, into northern China. During the last few years before the outbreak of the Sino-Japanese War the Japanese constantly looked for weak spots in the Nationalist government's hold on northern China. They formed several short-lived local governments within the demilitarized zone and in the remote Chinese provinces of Chahar and Suiyuan. Between 1935 and 1937 fighting also took place in the outlying Chinese province of Suiyuan when 'proxy' Inner Mongolian forces attacked several towns. The poorly trained Inner Mongolians were supplied with Japanese arms and undercover Imperial army officers advised the rebels. Japanese troops in Mongolian uniforms also operated tanks and artillery donated to the Inner Mongolians, while pilots flew a handful of planes for them. Although the Mongolians were surprisingly beaten by the local Chinese troops, their withdrawal was temporary and they returned at the start of the Sino-Japanese War.

The Nationalist army that prepared to meet any further aggression by the Japanese in 1937 was a large force of approximately 1,700,000 regulars and 518,400 reservists. It was almost entirely an infantry force with only one or two mechanized units equipped with a few tanks and armoured cars. Artillery was in short supply with most guns being leftovers from the 1920s and only a few dozen modern guns imported from Germany, Sweden and other European countries. Loyalty to the central government of Chiang Kai-shek amongst large sections of the army was questionable with only 380,000 troops described as being 100 per cent loyal. A further 520,000 troops belonged to units which although 'traditionally loyal to Chiang', could not be totally counted on. The rest of the army was a mixture of units loyal first and foremost to their commander or units that were 'politically' doubtful.

A typical, exotic-looking Chinese Nationalist soldier fighting the Japanese in Manchuria in 1932 is pictured before going out on patrol. His sheepskin hat and padded uniform are well adapted to the severe weather of the 1931–2 fighting. With a MP-28 sub-machine gun over his shoulder, he looks resolute enough but the odds were against the Chinese defenders. A lack of any real support from the government in far-off Nanking meant that the struggle against the Japanese was in the end futile.

A Japanese Imperial army mountain gun fires towards positions held by Chinese troops in the northern Chinese province of Manchuria in 1931. The Japanese had been gradually increasing their influence in Manchuria since their victory over the Chinese in the First Sino-Japanese War (1894–5). In 1931 they made their first major land grab of Chinese territory with the invasion of Manchuria. Within a few months they had set up a client state called Manchukuo which they effectively ruled through a puppet emperor until August 1945.

Japanese troops guard one of the Nationalist armoured trains captured during fighting in Manchuria between 1931 and 1933. The fleet of armoured trains in Manchuria belonged to the Nationalist North-Eastern Army of Chang Hsueh-liang. Most of the captured trains were repaired by the Japanese and used on the open plains of Manchuria and northern China until August 1945.

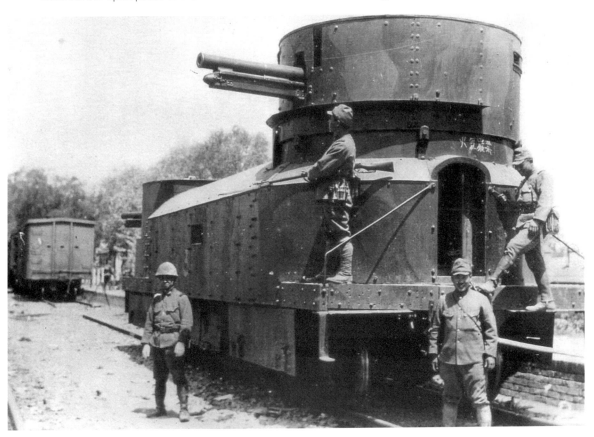

Chiang Kai-shek, the 'Generalissimo' of Nationalist China, ruled the country from the late 1920s. He had faced opposition from the Chinese Communists since he took power and open aggression from the Japanese empire since 1931. When full-scale war broke out between China and Japan in 1937 Chiang proved a stubborn leader. He was not willing to surrender to the Japanese even in the face of heavy defeats or to come to terms with them as they expected.

In a pre-war manoeuvre a Chinese Nationalist Vickers 6-ton light tank armed with a 37mm Puteaux gun moves along a road. Modern armoured vehicles like this were imported by the Chinese in the 1930s but never in sufficient numbers to form large mechanized units. The Nationalists suffered from a confused purchase policy which saw several types of tank imported.

Nationalist artillerymen practise with rangefinders during training in the year before the outbreak of the Sino-Japanese War. The more successful Nationalist units received the best weaponry and equipment leading to a sharp contrast between the best and worst Chinese divisions in 1937.

Soldiers of the Nationalist army on parade to celebrate the fiftieth birthday of their leader Chiang Kai-shek on 30 October 1936. They are parading in the southern city of Canton which Chiang was visiting for the first time in ten years. Canton had been the original base of the Kuomintang Party and its Nationalist army which defeated the Chinese warlords between 1926 and 1928. Men on the right of the parade are armed with Daido fighting swords worn in scabbards on their backs.

By 1936, when this photograph was taken, Chiang Kai-shek was supposedly the undisputed leader of Nationalist China. He is seen in discussions with General Lung Yun, the 'wily' governor of Yunnan from 1927 who ran his province more or less as his own fiefdom. Lung's loyalty to Chiang was always uncertain and the Nationalist leader could never really trust him. Unfortunately for Chiang, there were many of his generals and their troops, especially in the outlying provinces of China, whose support was questionable.

General Pai Chung-hsi, the leader of the Nationalist troops in Kwangsi province and one of the commanders who proclaimed his intention to fight against the Japanese in 1936. Many of the independently minded Nationalist commanders ran their provinces in the same way as they had in the warlord era of the 1920s. Pai had rebelled against Chiang Kai-shek several times in the 1930s and although allowed back into the Nationalist fold, had little loyalty to his leader. He was one of the generals who were frustrated at the Nationalist leader's perceived 'appeasement' of the Japanese from 1931 to 1937.

Massed ranks of Nationalist Chinese troops march past the review stand in a show of force by Chiang Kai-shek's government in 1936. The Chinese were never short of manpower and in most cases the Nationalists could at least arm their men with rifles and basic equipment. It was when it came to modern heavy weaponry that the Chinese army revealed weaknesses that were not going to be corrected by 1937. These troops were just as likely to be fighting Communist or other rebellious elements within China as the Japanese.

After the formation of the 'United Front' between sworn enemies the Communists and Nationalists, these Red Army troops in Shensi march off to join the Nationalist army in September 1937. In theory the uneasy alliance would hold as long as China was threatened by the Japanese invader. In reality an undeclared civil war existed almost from day one between Chiang Kai-shek's and Mao Tse-tung's followers. The banner flown behind the Communist volunteers proclaims their support for the Republicans fighting their own civil war in Spain.

Two of the most prominent Chinese Communist leaders are pictured at their Yenan headquarters in the aftermath of the Long March of 1934–5. Mao Tse-tung, the leader of the party, had finally managed to consolidate his position at the head of the Communists during the Long March. Chou En-lai, in the cap, was the Political Director of the Red Army and was the main negotiator in talks with Chiang Kai-shek. His diplomatic skills when dealing with the Nationalists led to the United Front agreement to fight the Japanese in early 1937.

Communist machine-gunners are seen training with their Browning heavy machine gun before the war. These men belong to one of the better Communist guerrilla units which fought the Japanese after 1937. The civil war between the Nationalist government and the Communists weakened the Chinese ability to resist Japanese incursions into their territory. In the accompanying caption to this photograph its states that the average age of a Communist soldier was 19 in 1936.

Japanese youth volunteers assembled near Tokyo in the 1930s serve to demonstrate the empire's total preparation for war. The boys' headgear shows that they belonged to several organizations, all of which were designed to prepare them for military service. Japan was like Nazi Germany, a militarized state with military style uniforms worn by school children, students and many workers.

Like their male compatriots, the women and girls of Imperial Japan were brought up from birth to be prepared to serve their nation. The girls in the foreground belong to the Showa Association, the main patriotic organization in Japan in the 1930s. Public support in Japan for the war in China was almost total and the young girls and women of the empire played their part. Although their role in Japanese society was generally subservient, they were expected to fulfil many male roles when war began.

In this pre-war photograph the crew of a camouflaged Japanese Imperial army Type 95 75mm field gun prepare to fire their weapon. Based on the French Schneider Mle 1931, this gun was first made in 1935 and was intended to replace the Type 41, which dated from 1908. The crew are taking part in a large-scale manoeuvre and wear white hat bands as a field sign to distinguish the competing armies.

Soldiers of the Japanese Imperial Guard march through Tokyo in a pre-war parade in front of Emperor Hirohito. The Imperial Guard was established in 1871 exclusively from ex-Samurai warriors and remained an 'elite' formation. However, it had not fought in action since 1905 and was not to do so until the Pacific Campaign of 1941–2. Most of the Japanese Imperial army was far less concerned with the 'spit and polish' of the parade ground and fighting capability was its major concern.

Japanese Emperor Hirohito posing in his full dress uniform for an official portrait in the mid-1930s. The emperor, who had acted as regent since 1922, came to the throne in 1926 and was formally enthroned in 1928. Although worshipped by the Japanese people as a god, in reality his power in modern Japan was largely symbolic. His status is perhaps best explained by saying that Japan was not ruled 'by' the Emperor but in the 'name' of the Emperor. This symbolic status does not excuse his role in wartime Japan and how much responsibility he had for the war against China and the Allies is open to debate.

Soldiers of the Inner Mongolian Army which fought a 'proxy' war against the Nationalist government in Suiyuan province in 1936. Before the outbreak of the Sino-Japanese War in 1937 the Japanese supported several rebel groups in China that were willing to fight Chiang Kai-shek. The Inner Mongolians were fighting for a separate state in Suiyuan and Chahar provinces and received small arms, artillery and clandestine air support from the Japanese. These same troops were to join the Japanese advance through their region in September 1937 serving as irregular cavalry.

Tough-looking soldiers from northern China pictured during fighting against Mongolian rebels in late 1936. They had fought in an undeclared war between the Nationalist government and the Japanese and their Chinese 'puppets' in the remote provinces of Chahar and Suiyuan. Although the Chinese had been largely victorious, they were soon to be overrun by the Japanese when full-scale war broke out.

In the last weeks before the outbreak of full-scale war between China and Japan in July 1937 a civil defence drill takes place in the city of Hankow. As the fear of a Japanese invasion of China increased more and more air raids and other drills took place. The Kuomintang Party organized its members into various first-aid, air-raid patrol and firefighting forces in preparation for the coming conflict.

A Nationalist mountain howitzer being used in a pre-war manoeuvre with the crew sheltering underneath camouflage netting. The gun is an imported Swedish Bofors 75mm M1930 model, one of the few modern types used by the Nationalist army at the start of the war. There were never enough artillery pieces in the Chinese army and most guns were kept under the strict control of commanding officers. One of the Nationalists' greatest weaknesses was their fear of losing precious weaponry in battle. For this reason some guns were kept at divisional headquarters instead of at the front line where they were needed.

有我無敵！有敵無我！
軍委會政治部

This Nationalist propaganda poster of the Sino-Japanese War has the 'brave' and athletic Chinese soldier killing the 'cowardly' and animal like smaller Japanese soldier who cowers in fear. Racial stereotypes were used widely by both sides in this brutal war with the intention of de-humanizing the enemy.

Chapter One

The Outbreak of War, July–October 1937

The 2nd Sino-Japanese War between the Japanese empire and Nationalist China broke out on 7 July 1937. It began as yet another local clash between Japanese garrison troops and local Chinese units in the area around the famous Marco Polo Bridge to the west of Peking. Japanese troops had been on a night manoeuvre when firing began after the suspected abduction of one of their men. Usually these 'incidents' had been quickly settled, often with a humiliating apology from the Chinese side. This time a series of letters backwards and forwards between the two sides failed to reach a settlement. The Japanese demanded the withdrawal of the Chinese Twenty-ninth Army from Peking but this was rejected by the Nationalist government. On 27 July the Japanese's patience ran out and they advanced on Peking, taking the city the next day. The famed but archaic 'Big Sword' soldiers of the Twenty-ninth Army attacked the advancing Japanese bravely but were duly massacred. The situation had developed into full-scale war that engulfed northern China. The shape of things to come became apparent when the population of the town of Tungchow, east of Peking, attacked the Japanese who were stationed there. Tungchow had been set up as the 'capital' of the mini-puppet state of East Hopei in 1935. Japanese residents and soldiers were killed during the fighting and when Imperial army units arrived they proceeded to massacre the Chinese population.

The next city to fall to the Japanese was Tientsin, which after the events at Tungchow, was cowed into submission. Following the Imperial army's previous policy it would have been expected that they would now halt their advance. It was anticipated that they would break away the northern Chinese provinces now under their control and set up some kind of puppet government. With no peace treaty signed, the Nationalist government ordered a general mobilization on 15 August. At the same time, the Japanese began to reinforce their forces in northern China while fighting had broken out in Shanghai (see below, p. 000).

In the meantime, a Japanese Expeditionary Force based in Chahar province began to move southwards into the rest of Nationalist-held Inner Mongolia. This advance was aimed at securing the northern flank of the Japanese army, while also setting up a client state in Inner Mongolia on the same model as Manchukuo. Fighting on this new desert front was carried out mainly with large mobile cavalry forces on each side, including Inner Mongolian cavalry fighting for the Japanese. This little-known campaign finally swung in Japan's favour with the arrival of the Mechanized Division with fifty tanks and twelve armoured cars. The Japanese advance then continued from Inner Mongolia into Shansi province, held by General Yen Hsi-shan, the independently minded warlord with a 120,000-strong army. Although some of Yen's troops fought well against the Japanese, the provincial capital of Taiyuan fell on 7 November. During the fighting in Shansi, the Japanese suffered a rare reverse when attacked by the 115th Division of the Communist Eighth Route Army in September. The 115th was officially under the command of Yen His-shan but took up positions overlooking the Pinghsingkuan Pass. A large Japanese motorized column advanced confidently into the pass and was ambushed by the Communist troops, who killed over 3,000 of the enemy. However, locally significant Chinese victories like this were never going to stop the overall advance and Japan reached all their objectives in northern and north-western China by the end of November 1937.

At the start of the fighting in July 1937 the Japanese Imperial army consisted of the China Garrison Army. This formation had been stationed in northern China in various strengths since the Boxer Rebellion of 1900. As the fighting intensified the Garrison Army was swiftly reinforced and reorganized into three separate formations, the First Army, the Second Army and the Northern China Area Army. Over the border in the puppet state of Manchukuo was the Kwangtung Army, the units of which could be used to reinforce the Northern China Area Army. By November 1937 the Japanese Imperial army in northern China totalled about 280,000 men. At the start of the war Nationalist divisions in northern China were not the best formations in the Chinese army. The Twenty-ninth Army, which faced the brunt of the Japanese advance, was commanded by General Sung Che-yuan, who Chiang Kai-shek didn't trust. Chiang was loath to send reinforcements to northern China as he wanted to save his best German-trained divisions to defend his heartland in central and southern China. Chiang's paranoia about the loyalty of his generals meant that only the most loyal could hope to receive his full support. Northern China had been sacrificed to Japanese occupation by November 1937 as the battle for Shanghai took all the available Nationalist army men and weaponry.

Soldiers of the Nationalist Twenty-ninth Army are seen guarding the Marco Polo Bridge near Peking at the time of the outbreak of fighting with the local Japanese garrison. It was this formation that faced the initial Japanese attacks in what soon escalated from a local skirmish into full-scale war. On this occasion Chiang Kai-shek refused to back down in the face of Japanese aggression and both sides rushed reinforcements to the area. Despite half-hearted attempts at negotiation between local Chinese and Japanese commanders, the Sino-Japanese War had begun.

Nationalist infantry move up to the front line near Peking in early August to support the Twenty-ninth Army which was under Japanese attack. This column of troops are near to the Great Wall of China, just to the north of the former capital. Although wearing modern German steel helmets, the reality of the Nationalist army in 1937 is demonstrated by the long line of porters needed to carry supplies.

The caption to this Japanese propaganda postcard says that this unit are advancing towards Peking in August 1937. These troops were to skirt around the edge of the city in early August but the main Imperial army did not make their formal entry until 8 August. However, the garrison did not put up much of a fight and withdrew from the city before they were completely surrounded by the Japanese.

Chinese infantry and artillery moving up to the front as the local fighting between Japanese and Nationalist units escalates. What began as yet another incident between the Japanese stationed in northern China and local Chinese forces soon spiralled out of control. Despite attempts at mediation, the vicious but low-level fighting developed into a full-scale conflict. The horse-drawn artillery are pulling what appears to be a Russian 76mm M1900/30 medium field gun.

A Nationalist Chinese soldier is seen in the early days of the fighting against the Japanese in northern China. He is armed with a German made MP-28 sub-machine gun, one of the many types used by the Chinese in the 1930s. The soldier's peaked cap was usually worn by northern Chinese soldiers instead of the standard Nationalist field cap. Spare magazines for the sub-machine gun are carried in the leather ammunition pouches of the special harness worn on the soldier's chest. Soldiers like this usually had to face the might of the Japanese Imperial army with small arms and the odd piece of artillery.

Japanese Imperial troops perform a banzai at Langtang during the initial fighting in northern China in July 1937. The banzai was performed in celebration of the emperor and the soldiers are acclaiming 'May the Emperor Live for 10,000 Years'. In the early days of the war in China the Japanese soldier was overtaken with a patriotic fervour rarely seen in modern warfare. This zeal would sustain most soldiers through any hardship they suffered during the first victorious few years of the conflict. As losses mounted and with no end to the war in sight, this initial enthusiasm gradually began to fade.

Japanese troops crowd into a machine-gun position on the outskirts of Peking as the old capital city of China is taken by the Imperial army in late July 1937. The Chinese forces in the region were poorly organized and units were often mixed up with no central control of the city's defence. The Imperial army's North China Garrison Army had carefully laid plans for the taking of Peking. They swept around the city from the west and north and Chinese forces retreated through any gaps left by the advancing Japanese.

Chinese Nationalist cavalry near Paotingfu in northern China in October 1937. The cavalry was never the strongest branch of the Chinese army and was mainly employed in the plains of the northern provinces. The rapid advance of the Japanese in the late summer and autumn of 1937 saw northern troops of this kind swept aside. Columns like this were tempting targets for the Japanese aircraft which soon enjoyed total air superiority over China.

This patriotic label from a pack of firecrackers features the Nationalist army going into battle against the 'enemy'. The original label is brightly coloured with a green-coloured tank in the background and the red, blue and white Chinese flag flying over the troops. Nationalist propaganda had been highly effective against the warlords of the 1920s. When the war with Japan broke out posters and other visual propaganda was utilized to the full by the Chinese government.

Japan produced a series of coloured 'comic' propaganda postcards showing scenes from the Sino-Japanese War. These were issued to soldiers to send back to their loved ones, presumably to show that the war was 'great fun'. This particular example shows Imperial army troops scaling the Great Wall of China and performing victory banzais. The voice bubbles contain suitably patriotic phrases, the particularly Japanese comic content of which would be lost in translation.

Japanese soldiers man a trench protected by barbed wire at Wanping, south-west of Peking, in the first days of August 1937. The old capital of China had been occupied by the Japanese on 31 July after the defending Nationalist Twenty-ninth Army had withdrawn to Tientsin. Peking's population was relieved that the Japanese occupation of the city was orderly but this was unfortunately not to be the case in the ensuing months.

Fearful Chinese villagers in northern China welcome advancing Japanese troops to their village with refreshments. Even when the local Chinese welcomed the invaders with Japanese flags and friendly gestures, they were not guaranteed good treatment. It was important for the Japanese, especially in the early months of the war, that any thoughts of resistance by the people was quashed immediately. However, not all Chinese people were loyal to the Nationalist government and if the Japanese had been less brutal they might have garnered more support from anti-Chiang Kai-shek civilians.

A Japanese anti-aircraft gun crew fire their gun from a flooded emplacement outside Peking in late 1937. They are operating a Type 10 76.2mm anti-aircraft gun, which was produced from 1921 in Japan. This model of gun was usually operated by naval personnel and, although not clear here, the crew may well be naval landing troops. In the first few months of the war much of the Nationalist pre-1937 air force was destroyed.

A column of Italian-supplied CV33/35 tankettes move towards the front during the build up to the battles for northern China. These vehicles were designated as light tanks but with thin armour and armed only with two Breda 8mm machine guns they were of little combat use. The exact number of CV33/35s in service with the Nationalists is unknown but twenty of this type did equip units at Nanking.

Artillerymen of the Chinese Nationalist army are given instruction by their officers in the operation of the German-supplied L32 150mm field gun. As part of German exports to China in the late 1930s, a few modern heavy and medium guns were sold to the Nationalists. Germany also supplied the Chinese with a few artillery tractors to pull the new heavy artillery.

With fists clenched a Communist machine-gun crew pose at their headquarters at Yenan in Shensi province. According to the United Front agreed between the Nationalists and Communists after the Sian Incident of 1936, some of these men's comrades were fighting as regulars in the Chinese army. This Browning heavy machine-gun crew, like the majority of the Communist combatants, fought independently of their so-called Nationalist allies.

One of the few victories for the devastated Chinese in 1937 took place at the Pinghsingkuan Pass in Shansi province in September. An overconfident advancing Japanese column was trapped in a valley by the Communist 115th Division, which had recently moved out of its base in Yenan. In this propaganda photograph a Communist Browning machine gun is firing down into the trapped Imperial army troops. According to some accounts, the Japanese lost 3,000 men during the fighting, along with 100 trucks and other equipment. Although an isolated incident, this victory shows what might have happened if the Chinese army had exclusively employed guerrilla warfare from the start of the war.

A heavily laden Japanese machine-gunner marches into battle with his Type 11 light machine gun over his shoulder. He wears typical Imperial army summer uniform with a light khaki field cap, shirt and trousers. The young soldier has tucked a branch from a blossom tree into his pack probably to remind him of his homeland. The kit fastened loosely onto his pack includes a blanket roll and some kind of cooking pot.

A couple of Japanese crewmen operate a Type 92 70mm infantry gun, introduced into Imperial army service in 1932. Although the Type 92 could be operated by a two-man crew, officially a squad consisted of an officer and nineteen men to carry the dissembled gun and its ammunition. With a range of 2,800m, the Type 92 was a useful weapon for the Japanese, especially in the rugged terrain of China.

Japanese troops take a quick meal break during a lull in the fighting in late summer 1937. In most cases the Japanese soldier was well fed, although they were capable of surviving on a small amount of rice when food was in short supply. Typical field rations in the Imperial army were between 3.5 and 4.5lb per day, made up of rice, barley, fresh meat, fish and vegetables. Canned fruit was also issued occasionally and troops received vitamin pills when they were available. Cigarettes, sweets and, of course, saki rice wine were also issued whenever possible, along with captured items of food and drink.

Nationalist artillerymen in northern China practise with their German Rheinmetall 75mm M14 mountain gun. This gun was a leftover from the pre-Nationalist warlord armies of the 1910s and 1920s. Although not a modern artillery piece, the Chinese utilized any guns they could acquire from the various regional armies after the defeat of the warlords in 1928.

Japanese Imperial air force bomber crews are briefed before going into action in the early stages of the Sino-Japanese War. At the start of the war the main medium bombers in service with the Japanese were old and slow types like the KI-1 and KI-2, which, although introduced in the early 1930s, were out of date by 1937. These bombers were joined later in the war by more up-to-date models like the Mitsubushi KI-21 and G3M2s. When the Japanese became overconfident they did send bombers unescorted on several occasions and these were devastated by Nationalist fighters.

Chapter Two

The Destruction of Chiang Kai-shek's Armies, August–December 1937

After the Japanese Imperial army's relatively easy victories in northern China many thought that they would now be satisfied with their conquest. However, on 9 August a new front opened up when fighting broke out between Chinese troops and Japanese marines in Shanghai. The commercial hub of Nationalist China, Shanghai had seen fighting five years previously and this had ended in a treaty that favoured the Japanese.

With 30,000 Japanese civilians living in the city the Japanese garrison stationed there thought it had a right to defend its citizens. There was also a large number of other foreign residents living in foreign concessions there which would mean the battle would be watched by the world at large. The struggle for Shanghai was to spiral from the usual armed incident into one of the most destructive battles in the Sino-Japanese War. The initial force of 4,000 Japanese marines was soon reinforced with a further 20,000 troops by the end of August. Japanese attacks on the Nationalist troops stationed to the north of the city were thrown back with heavy casualties on each side. Chiang Kai-shek sent more and more of his soldiers into the battle as he proved his determination to hold onto Shanghai. These included some of his 'elite' German-trained and equipped divisions which were to be sacrificed in the battle.

There is no space here to describe the battle in detail but it was a brutal fight to the finish between the two armies. Japanese attacks against the Nationalist defenders in the city and on its outskirts continued to build in intensity throughout September and October. In all the Nationalists committed 71 divisions with a total of 500,000 men and some of their best equipment. Amongst this huge army were three of the German-trained divisions which were thrown into the 'meat-grinder' that was Shanghai. Equipment sent into Shanghai included most of the Nationalists' modern tanks imported from Britain, Germany and Italy and artillery from Germany.

As casualties mounted in the battle with no sign of either side giving in, more Nationalist troops were sent to the front. Some estimates of the Chinese casualties suggest that 130,000 troops had been killed by mid-October. Replacements for the soldiers killed in the early fighting were rushed out by Chiang to bolster the city's defences. These were not, however, up to the standard of the troops of the first Chinese divisions and the Nationalists began to lose ground. Although the Japanese appeared to be winning, the battle was inflicting unacceptable losses which they could not sustain. In total the Japanese had sent 300,000 troops into the battle with 40,000 casualties suffered and 9,000 killed. These losses, although far lower than those suffered by the Chinese, led to demands from Tokyo for the battle to be concluded. To break the deadlock in the battle the Japanese made a number of amphibious landings behind the Chinese lines. Defenders also had to endure almost continuous heavy artillery bombardments from the Japanese, who had a far larger number of field guns. With little to counter the Japanese artillery except suicidal frontal assaults, Chinese morale collapsed. By 7 November an orderly withdrawal of Nationalist units began but this turned into a rout as they feared being outflanked and surrounded by the Japanese. Many were ordered to retreat towards Nanking to join the garrison there but many deserted along the way.

After the withdrawal of the Nationalist army from Shanghai, the Chinese capital, Nanking, to the west, became the next target for the Japanese. Retreating Nationalist troops from Shanghai now joined the Nanking garrison, which swelled to 100,000 men. These disparate units were from various disorganized provincial armies which often clashed with each other. When the new garrison commander, General T'ang Sheng-chih, took over the city's defences on 26 November he sent many of the most unreliable units out of the city. The reduced garrison of 22,500 prepared the defences of the city as best they could but morale was low even amongst the better units. As the Japanese approached Nanking on 10 December they bombarded the city for 48 hours and General T'ang and his staff left the city. Deserted by their commander, the garrison panicked and many soldiers tried to cross the Yangtze River to escape the Japanese attackers. Hundreds died in their desperation and there were few defenders left to face the Japanese, who entered the city on 13 December.

The fall of Nanking was quickly followed by a massacre of its remaining defenders and general population, the scale of which has been rarely seen in modern warfare. At first the captured Nationalist soldiers who had survived the battle were rounded up and put in holding centres. After discussions between the Japanese commanders in Nanking it was decided to kill all soldiers and any men who were suspected of fighting in the city's defence. Most were shot by machine guns and their bodies thrown in the river or burnt, while others were executed in brutal ways. These included burial alive, bayoneting to death and beheading, often by competing Japanese officers who held contests to see how many they could kill. In total it is estimated that about 31,000 troops and male citizens of Nanking were killed in the days following the city's fall. While the Chinese soldiers were being killed by some soldiers, others were raping as many females as they could get hold of. A large number of these incidents were mass rapes with the victim either dying as a result or simply being executed when the soldiers had finished with them. Although the extent of the slaughter is still contested by some Japanese historians and veterans, it is only a matter of how many thousands were killed. There were however a number of European witnesses to the massacre and all of these agree that the scale of the slaughter was enormous. Estimates of the number of victims over a 6-week period range from 6,000 to over 200,000. One Japanese expert claims that the slaughter numbered 42,000, while the highest Chinese estimates are 300,000! If the slaughter was organized with the intention of cowing the Chinese into submission it failed. Chiang was approached about coming to some kind of peace with the Japanese at this time but renewed his determination to continue the struggle.

Forlorn looking Nationalist troops take up their posts in the Shanghai region before a Japanese attack in autumn 1937. They have little to defend themselves with apart from their rifles and the light machine gun held by the man on the left. Other photographs of these troops show that they are armed with Mauser rifles and the machine-gunner has a Swiss-designed KE-7 light machine gun. The Chinese army was the only major customer for this weapon and bought over 3,000 and it was also produced in an arsenal in Szechwan province.

The crew of a Nationalist Hotchkiss M1914 medium machine gun prepare to fire from the cover of a pit protected from air attack by camouflage netting. Hotchkisses sold to the Chinese by the French were fed with strips of bullets from the left side of the gun by the loader. All of the crewmen have British-supplied MKI steel helmets, one of a number of models worn by Nationalist soldiers.

Moving slowly over a damaged bridge on the approaches to Shanghai, this Type 89A medium tank is followed by supporting infantry. This dramatic image shows the Japanese capability to advance over most obstacles in their offensives in China in 1937. The Type 89A was a tank that had been developed from foreign models imported by the Japanese in the late 1920s. It was a slow vehicle with a top speed of only 15mph, while most medium tanks of the period were about 10mph faster.

This cover of a photo news magazine published in 1937 shows the bugler of one of the German-trained Nationalist divisions. He wears the German M1935 steel helmet with a light khaki cotton uniform, issued to most Chinese troops. The ammunition pouches on his waist are to carry the clips for his C-96 automatic pistol, carried on his left hip. There was a large number of propaganda magazines like this produced in the 1930s to instil in the Chinese people a love of their armed forces.

A patriotic postcard aimed at the children of Japan shows boy soldiers proclaiming their loyalty to the emperor. The war in China was a popular conflict with the Japanese people who followed the exploits of the Imperial army, navy and air force avidly. Japanese children played war games at school with cardboard tanks and artillery and wooden rifles. They read stories of soldiers who died joyfully for the emperor and wanted to emulate their older male relatives.

Naval landing troops of the Imperial Japanese navy have set up a barricade in the middle of a road in the centre of Shanghai during fighting for the city. The position is obviously in a relatively safe section of the city as the troops are open to attack from the flanks. An officer directs his men from a standing position behind them and passes on his orders to the NCO laid prone in front of him.

Looking like medieval Samurai warriors, these Imperial Japanese army officers wear metal body armour at the front line in 1937. Breastplates were sometimes issued to snipers, engineers and other personnel who had to work in exposed positions. Presumably, the three officers wearing the armour are deemed to be in particular need of protection while visiting their troops.

A couple of young Nationalist soldiers pose during a break in the fighting for Shanghai in typical battle gear. The shorter man, wearing the light khaki uniform, is conventionally armed with a Mauser rifle. His comrade has not been fortunate enough to be issued with a rifle yet and has to make do with a 'da-dao' fighting sword and several stick grenades. Although deadly looking, the sword would only be useful at close quarters in the street fighting for the city.

This widely seen image of a grenade thrower of the Nationalist 88th Division in Shanghai shows the determination of the Chinese soldiers of 1937–8. Huge Chinese losses suffered in the bitter fighting for the city decimated the best Nationalist divisions. Their remnants retreated in front of the Japanese advance with some making the garrison of the Nationalist capital at Nanking.

An Imperial Japanese army Type 94 K light tank moves across the rough terrain during fighting in the suburbs of Shanghai. Japan's light armoured vehicles were virtually obsolete by 1937 but were faced by a smaller Chinese tank force. Armed only with a machine gun in its turret, the Type 94 continued to serve the Japanese during the Second World War.

During fighting in the Shanghai sector in 1937 these Nationalist troops are making an assault across one of the many waterways around the city. Their equipment and weaponry are fairly standard with a Browning heavy machine gun at the front of their assault boat. The helmets worn by the men are a model seen mainly in the fighting for Shanghai and were probably manufactured locally.

Devastating scenes like this on the streets of the Chinese quarter of Shanghai were to be repeated throughout China. The Chinese Nationalist air force was outnumbered and outclassed in the fighting over China in 1937. On paper the Nationalists had a fairly large air force at the start of the Sino-Japanese War, but poor maintenance and high attrition meant that few fighters were available to resist the Japanese bombers.

A Japanese light bomber drops its bombs over Shanghai in the midst of the crucial battle for the city. In 1937 the Japanese Imperial army and naval air arms flew aircraft that by European standards were slightly outdated. However, the real weaknesses of the Japanese air arms were not to be revealed until they faced the rapidly expanding Allied air forces after 1941. This Yokosuka B3Y1 was one of eighteen of this type operated by the Imperial navy over Shanghai in 1937. The plane was slow and cumbersome and had a poor reputation and was withdrawn from front-line service by the end of the year.

Japanese troops fire their rifles and light machine guns from behind an improvised strongpoint. The troops have opened up holes in the wall alongside steps up to an apartment building in the centre of Shanghai. Although Chinese losses in the battle for Shanghai were enormous, the Imperial army also suffered an unacceptable 9,000 dead. Nationalist army resistance to the Japanese came as a great shock to the Imperial army and proved that the Chinese were willing to fight for their country.

This motorcycle and side-car combination is parked at an intersection in Shanghai with its machine-gunner's finger resting on the trigger of his Type 11 machine gun. The crew is made up of naval landing troops, who formed a large part of the occupation force in the coastal city. On the side car of their Type 97 Sankyo motorcycle is a rising sun with rays insignia which shows that it is a naval vehicle. Naval landing forces personnel wore a green uniform with the Imperial anchor on the front of their steel helmets.

A Japanese artillery battery commander and his assistant operate a forward observation post in autumn 1937. They are using the model 93 battery telescope and binoculars from cover to check the range of their guns during fighting around Shanghai. Both men wear the M32 steel helmet which had a reputation for giving inferior protection to the wearer.

防敵偷渡之我哨兵

This patriotic cigarette card from 1937 exhorts the Chinese troops to resist the Japanese aggression. During the early fighting in China imagery like this was used to stir up the people who still believed at that time that the Nationalist government could defeat the invaders in conventional battle.

A trench full of Nationalist troops defending Nanking prepare to face a Japanese attack armed only with Mauser rifles. Although most of the German-trained and equipped divisions had been destroyed in the battle for Shanghai, some had withdrawn to Nanking. In total, the German military mission trained eight divisions of Nationalist troops between 1933 and 1938. The mission of seventy advisors was withdrawn by Hitler for political reasons in 1938, and plans to train a twenty-division-strong force were cancelled.

This image symbolizes the desperate situation of the Nationalist garrison at Nanking as the Japanese army advanced towards them. On the approaches to the Nationalist capital the defenders have built a few wooden and canvas fake tanks. Most of the 'real' Chinese tanks had been captured during the fighting for Shanghai a few weeks earlier and these mock-ups would fool no one.

In this brutal image from the aftermath of the fall of Nanking a Japanese officer prepares his Chinese prisoner for execution. The killing of thousands of Chinese soldiers and civilians during the Japanese invasion only served to stir up resistance. With nearly all Nationalist prisoners facing death if captured, many chose to fight on when surrender was not an option.

Chinese civilians tied to bamboo posts plead vainly for their lives with a Japanese soldier who is about to bayonet them. This tragic scene was photographed in the aftermath of the fall of Nanking in December 1937 and was unfortunately commonplace. First Nationalist soldiers then male non-combatants were slaughtered by the Japanese in the winter of 1937–8, followed by women, the elderly and children.

After the worst excesses in Nanking had ended, the centre of the city was cleared so that General Matsui Iwane could lead his troops in a victory parade. Matsui, the commander of the Shanghai Expeditionary Force, had been called back into service at 60, having retired in 1933. After the war the so-called 'Butcher of Nanking' was held responsible for his troops' brutal behaviour when the Nationalist capital fell. He was tried by the International Military Tribunal for the Far East, found guilty and then hanged in Tokyo in 1948.

Chapter Three

'The Decisive Year', January-June 1938

On New Year's Day 1938 at a meeting in the city of Wuchang Chiang Kai-shek reiterated his determination to continue the fight against Japan. He declared that from now on he would concentrate fully on the war and devote himself entirely to military affairs. The fall of Nanking in December meant that a new Chinese capital had to be established at Hankow in Hupeh province in late December 1937. Hankow, with its sister cities of Wuchang and Hanyang, made up a tri-city region known as Wuhan, industries of which were vital to the Nationalist war effort. For much of 1938 the focus of both the Japanese Imperial army and the Nationalists was Wuhan. The Japanese hoped that the capture of Wuhan would be the final straw for the Nationalists and that they would then sue for peace. Before the Japanese could begin their advance on Wuhan, however, they would have to defeat another large Nationalist army in Shantung province. The city of Hsuchow was defended by this large concentration of Nationalist divisions in the south-west of Shantung province. The battle of Hsuchow was one of the three most important battles of the pre-1942 period of the war. It involved a 240,000-strong Japanese force of 8 divisions and a 400,000-strong Nationalist army made up of 63 under strength divisions. The Nationalist divisions were made up largely of provincial troops who received little support from Chiang Kai-shek and his command. Before the battle commenced the Nationalists were fatally weakened by the unwillingness of one of their main commanders to fight. The general, who commanded 80,000 troops, withdrew when the Japanese attack began taking his silver coffin with him!

In March 1938 the Japanese occupied northern Shantung province, north of the Yellow River, and began to attack the Nationalist defence line along the southern bank of the river. Once the Nationalist defence lines had been breached, the Japanese moved southwards towards the city of Taierhehwang, which they reached in April 1938. It was here that the Japanese suffered one of their most humiliating defeats in the whole of the Sino-Japanese War. General Li Tsung-jen, the commander of the Nationalist troops in the 5th War Zone, masterminded the victory. In two weeks of fighting the Chinese basically drew the attacking Japanese force into a huge trap. Most of the Chinese troops were from the province of Kwangsi and had earned a good reputation during previous fighting. Beginning on 24 March, the Japanese 10th Division was lured into Taierhehwang, where vicious street fighting took place. As the fighting for the city continued, Nationalist divisions in the vicinity were rushed to the battle. These overwhelming Nationalist forces were then deployed to the city and in a well-organized enveloping movement surrounded the Imperial army units. By 7 April, when General Li announced his victory to the world, the Japanese had suffered approximately 14,000 casualties with only 2,000 escaping the city. For once the Nationalist command worked in unison and Chiang Kai-shek was credited with giving the defenders all the support they needed.

Although the victory at Taierhehwang was welcome, it did not in the long run affect the campaign for the capture of Hsuchow. The fighting for Hsuchow continued into May with the Japanese's mechanized units rapidly outflanking the city's defenders. By the middle of the month Chiang had decided that Hsuchow was going to be lost and ordered any units that could to withdraw before they were totally surrounded. Previously disciplined Nationalist units now lost their morale and retreated from Hsuchow, leaving the city to its fate. By 20 May, as the Japanese entered Hsuchow, the surviving Nationalist armies were moving south-westwards towards Wuhan. The battle for Hsuchow had lasted from 24 March to the end of May and left the Chinese army in central China in full retreat. Nationalist casualties in the Hsuchow Campaign were reported to have been 100,000, with the Japanese also losing 30,000. When the retreating Nationalists reached the mountain range around the tri-city of Wuhan they took up new positions and waited for the Japanese to move against them.

In June 1938 the Nationalist government made a decision that showed their desperation to stop the Japanese advance as well as their ruthlessness. Chiang Kai-shek ordered the dykes holding back the waters of the Yellow River to be broken, which would result in the flooding of vast tracts of land. Chiang and his leadership's rationale was that this act was an acceptable part of their 'scorched earth' policy. While acknowledging the suffering that would result, they argued that the survival of China was worth the sacrifice.

When the dykes were blown massive amounts of water flowed over three provinces, killing thousands and destroying crops and livestock before entering the sea south of the Shantung Peninsula. This desperate Nationalist plan was an attempt to halt the Japanese attack on Wuhan and in this it failed. What the flooding did do, however, was to kill thousands of Japanese troops and disrupt their military preparations. In addition, civilian deaths were enormous with a total of 835,000 people reported killed in the initial disaster. Many thousands more who survived the actual flooding suffered as refugees with no food and shelter and the death toll reached about 4 million. The sacrifice made by so many Chinese was in vain as the Japanese simply changed the direction of their advance on Wuhan.

The Nationalist army's losses in the fighting of 1937 meant that new recruits had to be found to fill the depleted ranks. These young men, escorted by an officer, could be volunteers for the army but often forced conscription took place. As a consequence of the crisis facing the Chinese these men would be given minimal training and pushed straight into the front line, sometimes without a rifle in their hands.

New recruits for the Nationalist army undergo training during 1938 as the Chinese government attempts to replace the losses of 1937. Although the large Chinese population meant that new volunteers could always be found, the quality of the training they received was not good. The Nationalist army remained what it had always been, an infantry force with a few small, mechanized and artillery units supplied largely by imported weaponry.

Hua, a 24-year-old Chinese resistance leader, is displayed by her Japanese captors like a living hunting trophy. The young woman was in command of a unit of fighters in Anhwei province in early 1938 when she was taken prisoner. Although she must know her eventual fate at the hands of the Japanese, she looks defiantly into the camera. Shortly after this photograph was taken she was executed as an example to any Chinese willing to resist the Imperial army.

A happy Nationalist soldier poses for the propaganda cameraman as he shoulders his Type 24 heavy machine gun. The major defeats suffered by the Nationalist army during 1938 badly affected the morale of its troops. Any army facing a series of almost continuous and devastating defeats would have lost its will to resist. For most soldiers, though, there was little alternative but to carry on fighting as neither side took prisoners in the brutal war.

A Nationalist artillery crew fire their Soviet-supplied M1902/30 76mm field gun towards Japanese positions. Russian artillery was supplied to the Chinese in the late 1930s, along with tanks, armoured cars and aircraft. The M1902/30 was a modernized version of the M1902 and was still in service with the Red Army. China was grateful for any heavy weaponry it received in the Sino-Japanese War. This was especially the case when Germany and Italy withdrew their support for Chiang Kai-shek's government. The new friendly relations between Japan, Germany and Italy in the late 1930s meant that the Nationalists could no longer rely on the Fascist dictatorships.

A camouflaged Nationalist T-26 light tank is unloaded from a river boat, having been received by the Chinese from the Soviet Union. Armoured vehicles, artillery and aircraft were sold to the Chinese by the Russians to counter any threat by the Japanese to Soviet Asia. With its 47mm armament, the T-26 was the most potent tank in service with the Nationalists and roughly eighty were supplied in the late 1930s.

Japanese soldiers hoist the sails on a river junk they are using to patrol a river during a offensive in summer 1938. Both the Chinese and Japanese used the many rivers of China to transport men and equipment. During several large-scale offensives in 1938 the Japanese ferried large numbers of troops in junks and other river craft. Japanese naval vessels were also used alongside armed civilian boats to give support during these offensives.

When the Japanese began landing their troops in southern China in 1938 they were often faced only by local Nationalist militia. This unit in Kwangtung province is under the command of the local Kuomintang official. The soldiers are armed mainly with C-96 automatic pistols, homemade bamboo spears and the odd rifle. When nothing else was available these guerrillas would go into action armed only with the 'da-dao' sword made in local workshops.

Communist guerrillas armed with Czechoslovakian-supplied ZB-26 light machine guns man a trench. Above the men flies the flag of the Chinese Red Army, placed there obviously for the propaganda cameraman. Tellingly, neither of the machine guns has a twenty-round magazine which demonstrates the Communists' shortage of weaponry and ammunition.

During street fighting for a Chinese city in 1938 these Japanese troops have occupied an improvised block house built from bricks from surrounding ruined buildings. The soldiers who constructed it have made two firing points for riflemen at either side of a firing position for a machine gun. Some Chinese cities were abandoned by the Nationalist army during the 1937–8 campaigns, while other cities were defended street by street by determined Chinese garrisons which fought to the last man.

A Japanese infantry squad receives a ration of saki before going into battle during an offensive in China. The troops are wearing the summer weight cotton uniform with the M32 steel helmet, some of which have canvas covers attached. Several of the men are wearing their field caps with sun curtain attached underneath their helmets. While this gives them a rather ungainly appearance, the Japanese were more interested in practicality than smartness.

The Nationalist Chinese imported most of their weaponry from Europe during the 1930s, and they used most types of small arms and light artillery available on the arms market. This British-made Vickers heavy anti-aircraft gun was bought in small numbers by the Chinese and was added to their exotic array of weaponry. A lack of standardization in weaponry before 1937 was one of the Nationalist army's greatest weaknesses.

This stylish Nationalist propaganda cartoon symbolizes the nation's support for the army fighting to protect them from Japanese aggression. Under the Nationalist flag a soldier, workman and peasant show their defiance to Imperial Japan. The Chinese made great use of posters and other propaganda images and towns and cities under Japanese threat were daubed with them.

An infantry section of the Japanese Imperial army moves cautiously forward behind the cover of a pair of light tanks. The Type 94 tankette was one of the most widely used armoured vehicles in Japanese service in China. Some infantry were formed into special 120-strong infantry tankette companies which operated with between 10 and 17 tankettes.

This close-up of a Japanese Imperial army machine-gunner shows the M32 steel helmet off to good effect. He is armed with a 6.5mm Type 3 medium machine gun, which was based on the French Hotchkiss design. Produced from 1914, its small calibre meant that it was underpowered and was in the process of being replaced by other Japanese models during the 1930s.

An artillery officer looks for the fall of his gun's shells during the bitter fighting for the city of Taierhchuang in 1938. This rare Nationalist victory was achieved by a combination of good leadership by General Li Tsung-jen and the overconfidence of the Japanese. At the decisive moment large reinforcements of troops were sent to surround the Imperial army trapped in the city.

During the Battle of Taierhchuang the Nationalists deployed a unit of these Cardon-Lloyd M1931 amphibious light tanks. The city was criss-crossed by waterways and these tanks helped to outflank the Japanese troops. They had advanced confidently into the city only to find themselves surrounded which required them to be supplied by air drop before making a chaotic retreat.

A long column of Nationalist troops captured in fighting in 1938 are marched to an uncertain fate. In the first few years of the war most of these men would be either executed or left to die of hunger. As the war progressed and the Japanese began to weary of the constant fighting, whole units of surrendering Nationalist troops were offered the alternative of joining a puppet army. Puppet troops fought their fellow Chinese alongside the Japanese Imperial army.

An exhausted soldier of the Nationalist army rests in the doorway of a house in the city of Taierhchuang. His commander, General Li Tsung-jen, became a Chinese hero after leading his troops to a hard-earned victory over the Japanese. Li took the advice of German military advisors when planning his battle before they were recalled to Germany by Hitler. Although the victory was rightly acclaimed by the Nationalists and their supporters, it was won at a heavy cost in both men and equipment.

The Japanese War Minister, Hajime Sugiyama (1880–1945), in the centre of the photograph pays a visit to the city of Woosung in May 1938. General Sugiyama was one of the 'hawks' in the Japanese military who demanded more troops be sent to China after the Marco Polo Bridge incident. After serving in various commands in China after 1937, he was eventually sent back to Japan to help prepare for its defence in 1945. When Japan surrendered, Sugiyama and his wife committed suicide rather than face life under Allied occupation.

A gun crew taking part in hard fighting in southern Shantung province against resolute Nationalist resistance in May 1938. The gun is a modern Type 94 75mm mountain gun, produced from 1934 with a range of 8,000m. Most of the crew wear the usual field cap, while their officer has the cork sun helmet worn in the heat of the Chinese summer.

Nationalist troops being transported to the front line in coal trucks on a small gauge railway take refreshments. They are on their way to Lungshai, where fighting took place on 21 May 1938, to replace heavy losses suffered by the Chinese. The shortage of arms at this stage of the war is evident by the fact that none of these reinforcements appear to have rifles. It was increasingly difficult for the Nationalists to replace both men and arms lost in the fighting of late 1937 and early 1938.

A long column of Japanese troops march, as the original photo caption says, 'towards an objective on the Tientsin-Pukow railway' in June 1938. The caption goes on to say that the soldiers have crossed a temporary bridge built by their unit's engineer company. As the Japanese advanced through China they were not only fighting against the Nationalist army but also against the terrain. Japanese support units performed well in keeping the infantry moving in the first victorious years of the war.

Two of the most prominent Nationalist commanders meet up to prepare for the defence of the vital city of Hankow on 22 June 1938. Despite their efforts, the city fell on 25 October, as did its twin city Wuchang after both had been evacuated by their garrisons. On the left is General Pai Chung-hsi, the 'Muslim General' and one of the so-called Kwangsi Clique which effectively ruled the Kwangsi province. The man to his right is the War Minister, Ho Ying-chin, one of the most loyal of Chiang Kai-shek's senior officers. Chiang Kai-shek could not rely totally on the loyalty of many of his generals, including Pai Chung-hsi. Like many of the Nationalist generals, Pai's first loyalty was to China not to the Nationalist leader.

A bodyguard unit of the Nationalist army waiting for a visiting dignitary in early summer 1938. The shortages faced by the Chinese army after 1937 are evident from the lacquered polo helmets worn by these troops. They are also all armed with C-96 automatic pistols which had been imported into China in huge numbers in the 1920s and 1930s. The smart woollen uniforms worn by the men instead of the usual cotton versions are another indication that this is a guard unit.

Chapter Four

'Delayed Defeat', July–December 1938

The Wuhan Campaign was probably the most vital of those conducted in the Sino-Japanese War. Chiang's ruthless decision to flood the Yellow River in June had in the short term prevented the Japanese from advancing southwards towards Wuhan. Instead, they planned to move up the Yangtze River valley to approach the tri-city region from another direction. Japanese forces gathered for this campaign totalled 380,000 men in 16 divisions making up the Eleventh and Second armies. A reflection of the importance of Wuhan to the Nationalists was the deployment of a force totalling 800,000 men in 107 divisions of varying strengths. Although the Chinese command claimed to be determined to defend Wuhan, their strategy was one of 'delayed defeat'. As one Western observer said, their plans amounted to 'delay, step by step withdrawal and defence in depth that presaged retreat and eventual acceptance of defeat'. It was to be the long-suffering foot soldiers of the Nationalist army who were to be sacrificed in this doomed defence of Wuhan.

Beginning on 10 June, the Japanese advance moved steadily along the Yangtze Valley. Some Nationalist formations fought well and the Japanese suffered a number of setbacks before the fortress of Matang fell on 27 June. Once this fort guarding any advance up the Yangtze River had fallen the Japanese could now use the river to support their offensive. After the fall of Kukiang on 26 July the Japanese advance was slowed, not by the Chinese but by disease. Dysentery broke out in the Imperial army's ranks but as their troops recovered over the next two weeks the Chinese lost an opportunity. The Nationalists were unable to exploit the Japanese weakness as their troops had their own problems with malaria in their ranks. Throughout August and September the Japanese continued their advance, destroying any Chinese forces standing in their way. The Chinese tactic of defence in depth was responsible for many of their defeats during the campaign. When the Japanese attacked along a narrow front the Chinese units on either side of the attack were prone to withdraw in disorder. Japanese casualties, however, were also mounting and in several engagements they lost ground to the Chinese. The 101st and 106th divisions of the Imperial army were even declared to be unfit for service and were withdrawn from the line. No matter what setbacks the Japanese suffered, however, their advance continued and by mid-October their columns were closing in on Wuhan. The tri-city region finally fell on 25 October and thankfully the terrible events at the fall of Nanking were not repeated. Estimates of Nationalist losses in the Wuhan campaign reached as high as 1,000,000, with the Kwangsi units suffering most. The disunity in the Nationalist ranks was revealed yet again as Kwangsi commanders blamed Chiang Kai-shek for his lack of support for their men. Huge numbers of Nationalist troops withdrew from the battlefield and reverted to guerrilla warfare. As with other conquests, the Japanese may have taken the urban areas but the countryside around Wuhan was still in Chinese hands. Japanese losses in the campaign, although not on the scale of their Nationalist foes, were unacceptably high at 200,000 killed or wounded.

As the struggle for the heartland of central China reached its last phase, the Japanese launched a further advance in southern China. On 21 October a Japanese amphibious force landed 70,000 troops and marines in Kwangtung province and captured the last major port, Canton. The garrison of Canton did not put up much of a fight and the Japanese occupied the port with little effort. Japan had already captured the southern ports of Amoy, Foochow and Swatow in May 1938 so the fall of Canton effectively prevented Nationalist China from importing supplies by sea.

With the fall of the industrial heartland of Wuhan and of the last major port of Canton, China was in a desperate situation. The Japanese, not without reason, assumed that Nationalist China was bound to fall or Chiang would have to come to some agreement with them. The Nationalist government, far from giving up the struggle, had been preparing for further resistance. Industrial facilities, universities and other government institutions had been moved westwards, away from the Japanese advance. In a miracle of organization the Chinese had evacuated 2,000 firms with their machinery and other equipment to set up mills, armouries and factories to the west. Chiang and his advisors had decided to move their capital to far-off Chungking in the western Chinese province of Szechwan. The city was one of the most undeveloped and remote cities in China and had been a hotbed of rebellious warlords throughout the 1920s. As commentators said of Chungking, its only possible advantage as a capital city was its remoteness from the rest of China. Although unsuitable as a peacetime capital, it was the only rational site for a wartime capital and was to serve as such until 1945. During the war the city's population was to swell from 300,000 to 1,000,000 as the civil service and military hierarchy of China was crammed into its overcrowded buildings. Defended by the divisions most loyal to Chiang, the city was safe for the time being from Japanese land offensives but not from the Imperial air force. Chungking was to become one of the most bombed places on earth from May 1939, when it came in range of Japanese air fields, until 1945.

Meanwhile, the Nationalist army in the rest of unoccupied China was still of a significant size, with 300 divisions on paper in late 1938. Some of these divisions, however, were under strength and poorly equipped. Most of the surviving divisions were widely dispersed around the few provinces still in Nationalist hands. They were often under the command of generals whom Chiang regarded as 'unreliable' and whose troops had little loyalty to the central government. It is truly remarkable, however, that the Chinese were still fighting after all the setbacks they had suffered in the 1937–8 campaigns.

A unit of Japanese Imperial army Type 94 tankettes cross a river during an advance into Nationalist-held territory in summer 1938. These light tanks were by far and away the most common type of tank in service with the Japanese in China. By this stage in the war most Nationalist tanks had been destroyed and the Type 94 was able to continue in use. When faced with Allied tanks in Burma in 1944–5 and the Soviet army's tanks in Manchuria in 1945, they were quickly destroyed.

Chiang Kai-shek and two of his generals inspect two armoured vehicles that have survived the early campaigns against the Japanese. Chiang Kai-shek is looking into the hatches of an Italian CV33/35 tankette with a Russian-supplied T-26 light tank in the background. Both types had been supplied to the Chinese during the 1930s and the vast majority of them had been lost in the battles of 1937–8.

Japanese artillerymen fire their Type 92 105mm field gun which had entered service with the Imperial army in 1932. This field gun was one of the more modern types in service with the Japanese during the Sino-Japanese War. Its crew wear one model of the cork sun helmet worn by the Japanese soldier in the summer as well as the tropical shirt and woollen breeches.

Thousands of civilians were killed in air raids on the temporary Nationalist capital of Chungking between 1938 and 1945. Shortly after Chungking became the centre for continued Chinese resistance in 1938, Japanese bombers began their relentless bombing campaign. Japanese land forces could not reach the isolated city in Szechwan province so the Imperial army and naval air forces were sent against it to try and bomb it into submission. These women and children have been caught in the open on one of the staircases that led from the city down to the river during a raid.

This impressive overhead photograph illustrates well the difficulties of moving heavy weapons and equipment over Chinese terrain. The artillerymen are struggling to drag two gun limbers up a slope with an eight-mule team and a total of twenty-three men with ropes to pull the load. With such huge distances to cover in their conquest of China, the ordinary Japanese soldier faced this kind of task on a daily basis.

The crew of a Danish Madsen M1930 light machine gun look to the skies as Japanese aircraft fly over a Nationalist-held city in 1938. Without anti-aircraft sights the chances of shooting down an aircraft with this weapon are slight unless it is flying very low. A couple of men from this rather over staffed machine-gun crew hold the gun stand steady but at least two of the crew appear to be surplus to requirements.

Nationalist militiamen from the Canton region rush to defensive positions armed only with roughly made spears in 1938. The south of China had remained largely loyal to Chiang Kai-shek and his government since the 1920s. These patriotic volunteers would soon face the invading Japanese and hopefully at least a few would be given rifles before going into action.

Nationalist infantry perform a river crossing in the summer of 1938 with ZB-26 light machine guns covering them. As with all troops trying to cross water, these men are extremely vulnerable if caught out in the open. By this time the Nationalist army had suffered very great losses and the replacement troops were not as well trained.

Japanese military policemen of the dreaded Kempei-tei carry out a search of Chinese civilians in an occupied city in 1938. The Kempei-tei were feared almost as much by the ordinary Japanese soldier as by the civilian population of China. They enforced a policy of strict discipline in the Japanese Imperial army and tortured and killed any Chinese willing to resist them.

Japanese Type 89 medium tanks trundle through an occupied northern Chinese city while the Chinese population look on. The Type 89 was a slow tank with a maximum speed of 15mph and was poorly armoured with a maximum thickness of 15mm. However, it was well armed with a 57mm gun and several machine guns and had first been produced in 1929. Although not a good design, the tank was more than adequate for the war in China as it faced little opposition from Nationalist armour.

Nationalist Chinese anti-aircraft gunners defend a city with their Italian Canone-Mitragliera da 20/65 Modello 35 during the fighting of 1938. This 20mm gun was one of a number of types of light anti-aircraft gun used by the Nationalists in the 1930s. Light guns like this made up the vast majority of anti-aircraft defences of Nationalist cities and were usually moved from location to location.

Chinese Nationalist flak gunners use their heavily camouflaged light anti-aircraft guns as light artillery in fighting with the Japanese. Although covered in foliage, the guns all appear to be Danish Madsen 20mm Model 1935s. The Madsen was one of the rarer weapons employed by the Chinese but was used by many of the smaller nations in the 1930s. One of China's greatest problems during the Sino-Japanese War was the wide variety of types of weapon in service.

Nationalist cavalry move across flooded land during a patrol in the no-man's-land between Japanese- and Chinese-held territory in 1938. The Nationalist army made little use of cavalry during the Sino-Japanese War even when the Chinese terrain was suitable for their use. All draught animals in civilian hands were usually confiscated by the Japanese, leaving a shortage of horses for regular cavalry on both sides.

A couple of Japanese soldiers on patrol in northern China have adopted a new type of transport well suited to the terrain. Camels were widely used in northern China as draught animals and sometimes were also seen in this role with the Japanese during the Second World War. Japanese troops were known for adapting to the country they served in and the use of camels in the desert made perfect sense.

A trio of Japanese soldiers stand victorious atop the fortifications on one of the many walled Chinese cities taken by them in the 1937–8 fighting. At this early stage in the Sino-Japanese War the morale of the Japanese Imperial army was high. Even though they achieved a series of unbroken victories against the Nationalist army, they did suffer heavy casualties. All three men are wearing minimal uniform in the heat of the Chinese summer, with two men in their undershirts. The junior officer in the centre of the group appears to have broken his katana sword blade during the fighting.

A long column of Nationalist troops marches down a road in central China in summer 1938. As with most Chinese units, their baggage is being carried by porters who are basically soldiers without weapons. If their comrades were killed or injured, the porters would then take up their rifles and join the front line. The steel helmets worn by the men are a model unique to the Nationalist army and were commonly worn during the early days of the war.

These prisoners are about to be executed with a single bullet to the back of their head by Nationalist troops in 1938. Japanese spies, Communist agitators and ordinary criminals could expect little mercy under Nationalist rule. Chiang Kai-shek's control of China in the 1930s and 1940s was total, with only a semblance of democracy. Under war conditions state paranoia meant that anyone suspected of threatening Nationalist rule could expect the same treatment as these two men.

Nationalist infantry crouch low as they rush past a pagoda to attack the Japanese during fighting in summer 1938. Although the Sino-Japanese War is usually seen as a unbroken series of Japanese victories, this was not always the case. The Chinese army fought the Japanese to a standstill on a number of occasions but their soldiers' sacrifices were in vain.

A Japanese sentry guards Chinese peasants as they bring in the harvest in the Shanghai region in summer 1938. The ordinary people of China often suffered terribly under Japanese occupation and these peasants were most likely forced to work for the Imperial authorities. The Japanese attitude to the Chinese was best summed up by the fact that many referred to the peasantry as 'so much wood' rather than as fellow human beings.

This Nationalist Maxim Type 24 heavy machine-gun crew are performing anti-aircraft drill in summer 1938. The crew are wearing German M35 steel helmets with their cotton uniforms and have motor goggles around their necks. They probably belong to one of the motorcycle units raised by the Nationalists to act as mobile anti-parachutist troops. Their relatively smart uniforms also suggest that these soldiers belong to an elite Nationalist unit.

A column of Nationalist troops move up to the front line at Hankow just before the fall of the city in late October 1938. Fighting for the twin cities of Wuchang and Hankow had been taking place since June and involved hundreds of thousands of troops on both sides. This unit is at Hsinyang, 135 miles north of Hankow, and the soldiers have camouflaged themselves with foliage against air attack. After heavy fighting the Nationalists evacuated both cities and the Japanese occupied them on 25 October.

Japanese Imperial naval landing troops watch the bombardment of Nationalist positions around the port of Canton in October 1938. The Japanese launched a series of amphibious landings in May 1938, taking most of the southern ports held by the Chinese. This left only Canton in Nationalist hands until the autumn when the city was taken by the 70,000-strong Twenty-first Imperial Army. Canton's garrison was made up of the Twelfth Army Group and cut off from aid it did not put up much of a fight against the Japanese.

The crew of a Nationalist air force Tupolev SB-2M 100-A bomber put on their flying suits before setting off on a raid on Japanese-held positions. Tupolev bombers and I-15 and I-16 fighters were supplied to China by the Soviet Union in the late 1930s. In total 292 of this type of bomber were sold to the Chinese air aorce and came with a number of Soviet advisors. Stalin's reasons for helping the Chinese with armaments and aircraft were purely pragmatic. Support for the Nationalists kept the Japanese occupied and diminished their perceived threat to the Soviet Union's Asian provinces.

Just before the fall of Nationalist-held Hankow in November 1938 this locomotive shunts forlornly around the city's rail yard. By the time this photograph was taken Hankow was completely surrounded by the Japanese Imperial army and this train is going nowhere. Even though they know this, desperate civilians climb aboard the locomotive hoping that somehow it will carry them to safety.

Nationalist troops take up positions during the long-running battle for Wuhan, the tri-city region made up of the cities of Hankow, Hanyang and Wuchang. In the 5-month battle for Wuhan about 800,000 Nationalist troops were employed against 380,000 Japanese. The industry concentrated around Wuhan made it vital that the Nationalists should hold onto the region. By late October 1938 the 3 cities were all in Japanese hands and the Nationalists had suffered nearly 1 million casualties.

Chapter Five

Japan Triumphant, 1939-42

After two years of hard fighting and a series of unbroken defeats the Chinese Nationalist government was totally demoralized by the end of 1938. The dawn of 1939 brought no respite for the Nationalists and in February Hainan Island, off the coast of southern China, fell to the Japanese. The Japanese wanted Hainan to use as a base for the bombing of China's southern provinces and to reinforce its naval blockade. Japan hoped that by stopping supplies getting into China the Nationalist government would finally come to a settlement. Nationalist guerrilla forces withdrew to the centre of the island where they met the strong Communist guerrilla force based there. In late April, Nanchang, the capital of Kiangsi province, fell to the Japanese, who had been attacking the city since mid-March. The city, defended by a 200,000-strong garrison, was surrounded by a 120,000-strong Japanese army.

At the end of 1939 the Nationalists hopefully launched their large but poorly organized winter offensive against the Japanese. Chiang had managed to gather a large force for this campagin, using 550,000 front-line troops and guerrilla forces. The offensive was spread across nine provinces and lasted for much of the 1939–40 winter before petering out in February 1940. Although the Nationalists did make some progress at a heavy cost, the winter offensive was ultimately a failure as they could not hope to hold on to what they had gained. With a shortage of artillery and other heavy weaponry on the Nationalist side, any units that did gain ground were soon bombarded into submission by superior Japanese artillery. Most of what little heavy equipment and weaponry the Chinese had was lost in the fighting and with thousands of newly trained troops killed Chiang Kai-shek knew his forces were shattered. At the end of the offensive in early 1940 Chiang determined that from now onwards any Nationalist offensives in China would be purely regional with nothing approaching the scale of the 1939–40 offensive. Although Chiang tried to keep his generals' morale up by talk of future attacks against the Japanese, he privately admitted that his army was no longer up to the task.

It was in fact the Communists who launched the next large-scale offensive against the Japanese between August and December 1940, although the main fighting ended in September. The so-called Hundred Regiments Campaign was aimed at the Japanese army in northern China and involved 115 regiments of the Eighth Route Army. In 1940 the Eighth Route was still officially a unit within the Nationalist army but received its orders from Mao Tse-tung rather than Chiang Kai-shek. With a total of 400,000 regulars and guerrillas, the Communist forces involved looked impressive on paper but the men taking part were poorly armed. Communist forces attacked railways and roads and targeted isolated Japanese strongpoints and forts. Fighting was heavy and the Japanese and their 'turn-coat' or 'puppet' Chinese troops who fought for them were defeated on several occasions by the Communists. Despite some successes, the offensive died out for the same reasons as the Nationalists had failed. The end of the campaign was followed by a Japanese counter-offensive which brutally punished the civilian population who had supported the Communists.

Another result of the Communist offensive was the heavy Japanese attacks on the Nationalist army which had not taken part. This led to resentment by the Nationalist command who were unhappy with the independent stance taken by the Eighth Route Army. The discord between the Nationalists and Communists resulted in the end of their uneasy alliance. The United Front alliance of 1937 saw an agreement for co-operation between the Nationalist government and the Communists. It included Communist units serving under Nationalist army command until the Japanese were defeated. In an incident in January 1941 the 15,000-strong New Fourth Army, one of the two main Communist formations serving in the Chinese army, clashed with Nationalists, which resulted in the deaths of up to 5,000 Communists. Any hope of future co-operation against the Japanese was now over and the Nationalists spent the rest of the war blockading the Communists in their Shensi base. Chiang ordered the official disbandment of the New Fourth and for the rest of the war the Nationalists and Communists fought their own independent campaigns against the Japanese.

The fighting continued throughout 1941. In May the battle switched to southern Shansi province and ended in yet another withdrawal of Nationalist forces after heavy fighting. In September there was a second attempt by the Japanese to take the city of Changsha and again the Chinese managed to push the Imperial army back. In autumn 1941 fighting continued and centred on the strategically important city of Chengchow in Honan province. The city fell to the Japanese on 4 October before being recaptured by the Nationalists on the 31st.

Throughout their war in China the Japanese had consistently ignored any criticism from the West and the USA. After leaving the League of Nations in 1933 the Japanese had carried on as if international condemnation of their aggression had no effect on them whatsoever. Although the USA had stayed neutral when the Second World War broke out in September 1939, its sympathies lay with the beleaguered United Kingdom in 1940. When Japan signed the Tripartite Pact with Fascist Italy and Nazi Germany in September 1940 relations between them and the USA deteriorated. Trade embargoes were introduced by the USA and these had a detrimental effect on the already weak Japanese economy. The embargoes gradually impacted on 75 per cent of Japanese trade and targeted 'strategic materials' vital to resource Japan. During 1941 the USA had also begun to establish firm links with Chiang Kai-shek as the threat of war with Japan gathered pace. In August the USA introduced an effective embargo on oil exports to Japan, which if enforced meant that conflict with the Japanese empire was inevitable. Also in 1941, the British were threatened by Japanese aggression in their possessions in South-East Asia and the USA sent military missions to Chungking. Despite attempts at negotiation, the Japanese were unwilling to withdraw from China and when on 7 December 1941 the Japanese launched their attack on the US Pacific Fleet at Pearl Harbor Nationalist China's single-handed fight against the Japanese empire was at an end. From now on the Sino-Japanese War was to become a 'war within a conflict', a sideshow of the Second World War. However, if Chiang Kai-shek expected to receive large amounts of military and other support from the Allied Powers he was to be disappointed as they had enough problems of their own for the time being.

Hainan, the large island off the southern coast of China, was invaded by a Japanese expeditionary force in February 1939. The Japanese amphibious force that landed in the north of the island was part of the same army that had taken Canton the previous October. Although the Nationalist garrison was quickly defeated, a large Communist guerrilla force in the interior of the island was to prove a problem for the occupying troops. Here a sentry stood on a rooftop looks out over one of the towns on Hainan a month after its occupation began.

A Nationalist machine-gun crew have set up their Czechoslovakian-made ZB 53 heavy machine gun in an anti-aircraft role in Hunan province in 1939. Throughout 1939 the Japanese launched offensives in Hunan aimed mainly at the provincial capital of Changsha. General Chang Fa-kwei, the Nationalist commander of forces in Hunan, complained that his struggle with the Japanese was being ignored by Chiang Kai-shek.

A Japanese Imperial army Type 94 'Te-Ke' tankette stops while on patrol in the street of a recently occupied Chinese city. Its crewmen are sat atop their light tank viewing the local population warily with Nambu Type 14 automatic pistols at the ready. Armed only with a machine gun in its turret, the Type 94 could not be described as a battle tank and was designed as an infantry support vehicle. Having just been in action, the crew have fixed foliage to the body of the tank which has a Japanese flag painted on the front.

The crew of a Japanese Imperial army Sumida M2593 armoured car, which has been fitted with rail wheels, salute troops guarding the line in 1939. These adapted armoured cars were used for patrolling the railways which connected the guard posts and forts built to protect the lines. As well as the six-man crew, other Japanese troops are sitting on top of the car where they are vulnerable to enemy fire.

Relatively smartly uniformed Nationalist soldiers of a headquarters guard pose proudly outside their base in 1939. The officer and his men have all been issued with rarely seen double-breasted winter overcoats. Most Chinese soldiers wore a padded cotton tunic and trousers in the winter campaigns. Nationalist soldiers also wore the Japanese winter coat whenever they took these from captured stores or from the dead bodies of their enemy.

A hastily raised Nationalist militia unit parades in Kwangtung province before going into action in 1939. The men and women who make up this unit are armed, equipped and dressed with an exotic mix of military and civilian items. Headgear includes a few M1 steel helmets, trilbies and workmen's caps, while only one man has a military tunic. Although a few men have rifles, others are 'armed' with nothing more deadly than a wooden stave and a bugle.

This squad with Type 97 81mm mortars prepares to lay down covering fire for an infantry assault in winter fighting. The Type 97 was the most modern type of mortar in service with the Japanese Imperial army and was used alongside the Type 11, introduced in 1922. All the Japanese soldiers wear typical winter gear with a lambswool hat worn underneath their M32 helmets.

Nationalist guerrillas operating just to the north of Hong Kong while the Colony was still held by its British garrison, 1940. A year later the fall of the city meant that any clandestine support that the Chinese received from the residents of Hong Kong was lost to the guerrillas. Men like this could not expect much in the way of support from their leadership in far-off Chungking.

Nationalist militia raised in Kwangtung province listen to a speech by a Kuomintang official in March 1940. At first sight the men look like typical irregular guerrillas but their officially issued overalls and arm badges show they belong to a 'regular' formation. They are armed with older versions of the Mauser rifle with the odd ZB-26 light machine gun visible in the crowd. It appears that some of the men at the back of the group have no weapons and would have been armed simply with bamboo spears, the intention being to supply them with rifles when these became available.

During a Japanese anti-guerrilla operation a mixed unit of light tanks and infantry deploy in winter 1941. The infantry wear a hooded winter coat over the top of their regular woollen uniforms. Captured weapons were employed by the Japanese and the machine-gun squad is armed with an ex-Nationalist ZB-26 light machine gun. Armoured support is provided by the three Type 94 light tanks, the machine guns of which will provide covering fire.

A battery of Japanese 105mm Type 92 field guns fires towards Nationalist Chinese positions in 1941. As the war in China progressed the role of the Japanese artillery changed as it was used more and more to suppress guerrilla activity from long range. They rarely faced counter bombardment from Nationalist or Communist artillery because of the shortage of guns in Chinese hands.

A Japanese flamethrower operator shoots flames towards the gate of a Nationalist-held city in 1941. That year the Japanese were consolidating their position in northern Kiangsi, southern Shansi and Honan provinces. In the build-up to start of the war in the Pacific the Japanese Imperial army remained on the offensive in China. Bringing the Chinese to battle was now more difficult as they had learnt hard lessons about trying to take the Japanese in set-piece battles. The flamethrower is the Type 93, which remained the standard model in service with the Japanese throughout the war.

This German-supplied PAK 35/36 37mm anti-tank gun, pictured in 1941 in Kiangsi province, is one of the few that survived the military disasters of 1937–41. By this date most of the remaining heavy equipment and weaponry in the Nationalist army was kept in reserve. Nationalist commanders had one eye on a renewal of the civil war with the Communists when modern weaponry would be at a premium.

Soldiers of the Communist New Fourth Army advance in single file past holes dug for mines to be placed in at a later date. The centre hole is for a large mine, while the surrounding four holes are for small trip mines and the whole thing would be covered with foliage ready to use. The New Fourth Army was officially a unit of the Nationalist army following the formation of the United Front of Communists and Nationalists against the Japanese. During the so-called 'New Fourth Army Incident' in 1941 armed clashes between Communist and Nationalist units broke the uneasy alliance. From then on any pretence of co-operation between the rival factions ended and both pursued their own war against the Japanese occupiers.

Chinese Nationalist scout cars are seen on parade close to the wartime capital Chungking in early 1941. These Sfz 222 scout cars were sold to China by Germany in the mid-1930s and are amongst a handful to survive the 1937–41 fighting. Armed only with machine guns, these light armoured cars were no match for the Japanese tanks in China. Heavy equipment like this was kept well away from the war fronts by the Nationalists in preparation for post-war fighting with the Communists.

Nationalist troops move a German-supplied PAK 35/36 37mm anti-tank gun into a new position along the Yangtze River in November 1941. This gun is the original wooden, wheeled version rather than the more common rubber tired model. The Nationalists had a total of 124 of this type of anti-tank gun in service at the start of the Sino-Japanese War.

Japanese engineers haul a field gun up a slope during fighting in south-western Shansi province in summer 1938. The Japanese Imperial army had to overcome the difficult terrain in large parts of China often using sheer muscle power to move heavier equipment. They utilized every type of draught animal during the campaigns in China and requisitioned any they came across, without offering compensation to the peasant owners. This particular 'elite' engineers unit had a reputation for moving equipment and weaponry at speed. According to reports, they always hauled guns and other heavy equipment at a 'dog trot' in action.

A Chinese Nationalist soldier shows a captured Japanese poison gas canister to the world's press. Poison gas was used by the Japanese against the Chinese army throughout the Sino-Japanese War. The unreliability of gas as a weapon when dropped or sprayed from aircraft was probably the only reason that the Imperial air force did not utilize it on more occasions. Figures for the use of gas by the Japanese between 1937 and 1941 show that it was employed 9 times in 1937, 185 times in 1938, 465 times in 1939 and 259 times in 1940. In 1941 there was a marked reduction in the use of gas with only 48 occasions listed but it continued to be used to some degree until 1945.

Japanese troops storm into the outskirts of the city of Changsha, capital of Hunan province, which was fought over three times between September 1939 and January 1942. The original Japanese offensive against the city employed 100,000 men but failed to hold Changsha. A second attack in September 1941 was reinforced by a further 20,000 Japanese troops but again was pushed back after heavy fighting. A few months later a final offensive was launched but again after yet another battle for the city the Japanese withdrew their forces.

Nationalist troops remove bodies from one of the underground air raid shelters built for the population of Chungking in 1942. A direct hit on any of the manmade shelters or caves used as makeshift shelters resulted in horrendous casualties. Life in the wartime capital of Nationalist China was tough, especially for the poor who had to rely on what was provided by the government. The richer citizens of Chungking had their own private shelters built for them in the grounds of their houses.

A young female volunteer of the Nationalists Women's Volunteer Corps is seen on sentry duty in Chungking in 1941. Girl volunteers were raised to help the regular army defend the wartime capital from the Japanese. Many recruits came from amongst the ranks of the thousands of students who had escaped the Japanese occupation. The volunteers wore cotton dresses and either a cotton side cap or a broad-brimmed sun hat, as seen here.

Massed ranks of officer trainees at the Central Military Academy at Chengtu in Szechwan province parade for their commander in 1942. Although the Allies were training Chinese troops in India and western China, the Nationalists continued to run their own military academies as well. Most Nationalist officers came from the higher classes of Chinese society and these men have been issued with smart uniforms not available to the vast majority of troops.

The crew of a Nationalist gunboat operate their deck gun against Japanese aircraft in 1942. After the initial fighting in 1937–8, the remnants of the Chinese navy saw little service, largely because of the total Japanese air superiority. Any Nationalist vessels that took to sea would face air attack and most remained hidden in small harbours or sheltered up rivers in southern China until 1945. Starting the war with fifty-nine vessels, most of which were gunboats and other patrol boats, the navy had to be rebuilt after 1945.

Chinese women labourers work to fill craters left after a bombing raid on an airbase of the famous Flying Tigers American Volunteer Group in March 1942. Before December 1941 this Nationalist Air Force volunteer unit was made up of US pilots who flew 100 US-supplied P-40 fighters against the Japanese. After Pearl Harbor and the entry of the USA into the war against Japan, the Flying Tigers were absorbed into the US Fourteenth Army Air Corps. Many of the 'maverick' US pilots were unhappy about this forced conversion of the Tigers into a regular US unit.

Nationalist troops celebrate a rare victory against the Japanese at Changsha and show off their 'war booty' in 1942. The soldiers pose with the body of one of their dead foes at their feet and are festooned in Japanese helmets, gas masks, flags and rifles. This third battle for the city began in December 1941 and ended in mid-January 1942 with the Japanese being defeated.

A couple of Nationalist soldiers are pictured wearing captured Japanese M32 steel helmets and mock firing the Imperial army Model 10 grenade launcher after the battle for Changsha in 1942. Fortunately, both soldiers have been told that the small mortar is not meant to be fired resting on the knee. The grenade launcher for some reason was known as the 'knee mortar' but if used in this way would result in a broken or fractured leg at the very least.

Chapter Six

China's Guerrilla War, 1937-45

One of the most brutal aspects of the Sino-Japanese War was the guerrilla war fought from the outbreak of the conflict in July 1937 until the final defeat of the Japanese in August 1945. The guerrillas fighting the Japanese were made up of Nationalists, Communists and other non-political patriotic groups. Other armed groups of bandits fighting the Japanese had no patriotic feelings at all and were only interested in any booty they could capture. In the first months of the war the Nationalist Kuomintang Party had organized irregular units to fight in support of the regular army. Any irregulars captured by the advancing Imperial army were instantly executed, although their regular comrades were subjected to the same treatment. When the Nationalist army suffered heavy defeats in 1937 and 1938 retreating soldiers often joined the guerrillas or formed bandit groups. The thousands of soldiers left behind by the retreating Nationalists had a few stark choices. They could join properly organized guerrilla groups, either Nationalist or Communist, or one of the local defence societies, such as the Big Sword Society. Many of these local defence organizations had been formed to defend their villages against warlord armies in the 1920s. Other disbanded soldiers joined bandit groups which attacked the Japanese as well as any Chinese regular forces that they encountered.

As the Japanese advanced and occupied more of northern and central China, Nationalist guerrillas began operating. These forces tended to be locally raised and commanded by Kuomintang Party officials. Many of these guerrilla groups could not be supplied by the central government, especially after the Nationalists moved their capital to remote Chungking in 1938. Any pro-Nationalist group which operated in the same locality as a Communist group usually found that they were under threat by their 'allies'. The better organized Communist guerrillas would often absorb Nationalist groups by removing their leaders. If the Nationalist commanders were unwilling to join their men in the Communist fold, they were eliminated. Some pro-Nationalist leaders were happy to join their former enemies because they felt they had been abandoned by their government. The Nationalist central guerrillas operated throughout occupied China but one of their main strongholds was in Shantung province, where 170,000 guerrillas were based. Although the central guerrillas continued to fight until the end of the war the Communists had by 1945 pushed them into small enclaves close to Nationalist-controlled areas.

When it came to guerrilla warfare the Communists had a distinct advantage over their Nationalist rivals. They had effectively been fighting as guerrillas since the formation of the Red Army in 1927. Tactics and experience learned when fighting the Nationalists in the early 1930s was to stand them in good stead against the Japanese. Much of the fighting by the Communists was done by their few regular formations, some of which were at least officially under the command of the Nationalists up to 1941. The regular Communist forces, including the New Fourth and Eighth Route armies, fought a large number of engagements against the Japanese after 1937. For propaganda reasons the Communists' claims about the level of their war effort were probably exaggerated. One of their commanders said that between 1940 and 1942 the two main regular Communist forces had engaged half of the Japanese divisions! Another claimed that the Eighth Route Army had launched six major offensives against the Japanese in the first six months of 1942 alone. Japanese reports did, however, confirm that the Communists were their main foe at least in northern China. Their reports often stated that the Communists would usually fight to the death and few ever tried to surrender.

In support of the regular units were a large number of irregular forces, known as the 'Ming-Ping' or militia. They assisted the regulars on operations but also fought their own low-level war against the Japanese. The strength of the Communist guerrilla force, or Ming-Ping, had expanded to over 2 million by 1944, but most of these were unarmed irregulars. Many of the guerrillas were armed only with crudely made spears and booby traps, mines and other improvised weapons like wooden cannon. They also had unsophisticated matchlock guns and cast-off modern guns handed on to them by the regular Communist troops. Usually, any up-to-date arms given to the Ming-Ping were those with little or no available ammunition. As more weaponry became available from captured arms taken from the Japanese, puppet troops or Nationalists, the Ming-Ping provided a ready-made reserve for the regulars.

From the start the Japanese Imperial army met the guerrilla threat with extreme brutality in an attempt to subdue any Chinese resistance. This approach often turned out to be counter-productive, however, as it gave both the fighters and the general civilian population little in the way of options. They could either actively support the guerrillas and face any retribution meted out by the Japanese or try and keep out of the war. When the civilian population were punished, whether or not they aided the guerrillas, many decided they had nothing to lose by helping them. In addition, some guerrillas punished any civilians who did not actively support them and local leaders would be executed as an example to others.

The Japanese employed a number of tactics designed both to protect the territory they controlled and to destroy guerrilla forces. They safeguarded the lines of communication between cities, towns and villages with barbed wire, fences and stockades. Their engineers dug ditches and built strongpoints along the roads and railways and manned forts with small garrisons. In total, the Japanese were reported to have built 7,000 miles of fences and other obstacles to protect the railways and erected over 7,000 fortified posts.

Armoured trains and converted armoured cars ran up and down the railways between strongpoints to try and combat the guerrilla demolition squads that constantly tore up the tracks. Mobile columns were sent out on anti-bandit operations from Japanese-held strongholds in an effort to bring elusive guerrilla groups to battle. To try and surround the mobile guerrillas, the Japanese built stockades around the Communist bases which were gradually moved inwards towards their HQ. The Japanese columns criss-crossed guerrilla-controlled areas to push their units into a smaller and smaller perimeter. As the Japanese advanced they employed their policy of killing anyone they came across, as well as livestock. In this way they hoped not only to destroy active guerrillas but to cut them off from any hope of support from the local population.

One policy that the Japanese hoped would assist them in controlling China was the raising of 'puppet' units to fight for them. Since 1937 they had formed governments in northern and central China which were staffed by local collaborators. These puppet states were given titles, such as the Provisional Government at Peking in 1937 and the Reformed Government at Nanking in 1938. In 1940 a central puppet government was formed which officially united all previous governments under the former Nationalist leader Wang Ching-wei. The so-called Reorganized Government had its capital at Nanking and claimed to be the 'true' Nationalist government of China. It was 'allowed' or forced to recruit an army, navy and air force to fight alongside the Japanese against the guerrillas. In total the so-called Nanking Army reached a strength of 300,000 regulars with a small number of tanks and artillery pieces. Other local 'puppet' troops added several hundred-thousand to the official strength of pro-Japanese units, although these were totally unreliable. Nanking Army units went out on anti-guerrilla operations with Japanese units and performed reasonably well under their supervision. When fighting independently, however, they usually avoided combat with the guerrillas and often provided them with weapons and ammunition. Most puppet soldiers had no loyalty to Wang Ching-wei or the Japanese and many were absorbed into Nationalist and Communist units in August 1945.

A pro-Nationalist Chinese guerrilla fighter poses at his base along the southern coast of China. Even in the south of China, closest to Nationalist-held territory, it was difficult for fighters like this to get arms and ammunition. This man is well armed and has plenty of ammunition pouches on his belt, although they may or may not be full of clips for his Mauser rifle.

A Japanese signal unit in northern China uses dogs from the Canine Corps to transport carrier pigeons in wicker baskets. Imperial army signal units used the latest radio and telegram equipment alongside carrier pigeons, trained messenger dogs and couriers. As with weaponry, sophisticated communications equipment was withdrawn from China and sent to other theatres after 1941.

A mixed patrol of Japanese and 'puppet' Chinese troops take a break during an anti-guerrilla operation in 1942. The Chinese troops of the Nanking government, under the leadership of Wang Ching-wei, co-operated with the Japanese between 1940 and 1945. Wang, a former colleague of Chiang Kai-shek, became a puppet of the Japanese in 1939 and formed the so-called Reorganized Government in Nanking.

An elite unit of the puppet Nanking government's army marches out of its barracks to support its Japanese allies in 1941. At the head of the column is the flag of the puppet regime, which is almost identical to the Nationalist Chinese army flag. The only difference is the yellow streamer at the top of the flag, added at the insistence of the Japanese. The black characters on the streamer state the anti-Communist intentions of the Nanking government.

Anti-Communist, spear-wielding militia on parade in Shansi province as they co-operate with the occupying Japanese. Not all Chinese peasants flocked to join the Communists and members of several societies like the Red Spears actively fought against them. Only the commander on the right appears to be armed with a rifle and these men would be of little use to the Japanese.

Since the early 1920s armoured trains had been used in China by warlord armies, and many were captured by the victorious Nationalists in 1928. They joined those already in service with the Nationalists, who used them against the Japanese from 1931. Most of these were in turn captured by the Japanese Imperial army who used them to patrol occupied Chinese territory. This train appears to have been one of those in Chinese service and has Japanese-pattern camouflage added. Some were adapted by the Imperial army and fitted with Japanese guns and machine guns.

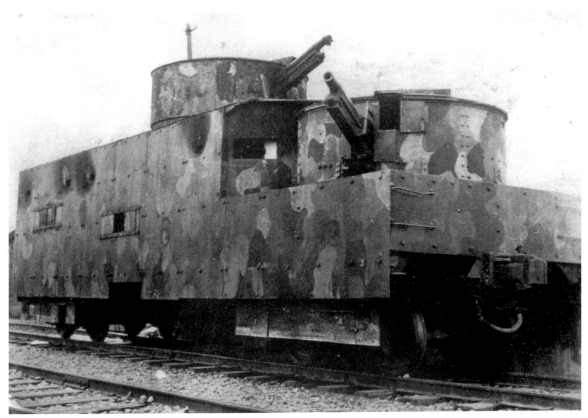

Japan's control of the railways of northern and eastern China was vital in keeping garrisons supplied. As the railways were under constant attack by guerrillas, armoured trains and vehicles ran patrols along them. This Sumida Model 93 armoured car has been converted to run along the tracks with specially trained troops aboard it. It was reported to take 10 minutes to convert this vehicle from a road-running to a rail-riding vehicle.

Japanese soldiers crowd aboard a rail workmen's truck as they move up the railway on patrol. Their role is to try and stop any destruction of the track by guerrillas or their civilian supporters. The rail network in occupied China was often protected by fences, barbed wire, strongpoints and constant patrolling by the Japanese army and Chinese puppet troops. The local population was often given responsibility for the section of the railway that ran past their village or town. If the railway was damaged, then village headmen or other leaders often paid with their lives as an example to the peasants.

Nationalist guerrillas aim for Japanese positions from their hilltop location in Chekiang province with a mix of rifle types. With no heavier weaponry available, the best that they could hope for is to fire off a few precious rounds and then withdraw. Although the men have no uniforms, they have written patriotic phrases on their bamboo sun hats. If a guerrilla or irregular was captured, the bruise left by the rifle butt on their shoulder would mean a death sentence.

Nationalist soldiers turned guerrillas gather outside their temporary headquarters during fighting with the Japanese army in 1941. On many occasions during the Sino-Japanese War large numbers of Nationalist troops were cut off by the advancing Imperial army. They had little choice but to continue to fight as guerrillas and many were absorbed into Communist groups before 1945.

A couple of young Nationalist guerrillas look nervously towards Japanese positions during an engagement in summer 1938. With just their rifles and a few rounds of ammunition they could only offer limited resistance to the advancing Imperial army. Along with thousands of their comrades, youths like these would be sacrificed in battle with the Japanese.

An elderly Nationalist guerrilla commander heads a unit of pro-Chiang Kai-shek irregulars in southern China. Most Nationalist guerrilla groups were led by local Kuomintang officials whose strength of personality often held their men together. They usually came into conflict with the Communists as much as with the Japanese and were often destroyed by their fellow Chinese, especially in northern China.

A well-uniformed and well-armed Communist unit put their Japanese Type 11 light machine gun into action in 1938. They have set up their machine-gun position on the heights overlooking a section of the Great Wall of China. By including the wall as part of the backdrop of their photograph the Communists give the impression that they control northern Chinese territory.

The Communist crew of this ex-German PAK 36 37mm anti-tank gun pose proudly with their rare piece of artillery. It is missing the shield but would be a welcome addition to the poorly equipped Communist forces. As with all Chinese heavy weaponry used in the Sino-Japanese War, replacing ammunition when supplies ran out was a major problem. The shells held by the crew could well be the only available for the gun so would be strictly rationed. They could not expect any ammunition from the Nationalist army unless they captured some from them.

Civilians are given some rudimentary training in defending their town against Japanese attack by Nationalist army officers in 1938. The young men and women of this group are armed with a few hoes and the odd rifle supplied by the army. If they tried to fight the ruthless Japanese Imperial army by themselves, their fate would be fairly grim. They would be better employed, like Communist irregulars, in attacking the Japanese supply lines.

A column of Communist regulars marches through a village and are armed to the teeth with Thompson sub-machine guns. The image is really an example of Communist propaganda as there was little ammunition available for these guns. They are copies produced in the arsenal of the Nationalist Shansi warlord, Yen His-shan. Because of the shortage of bullets for these weapons, later they had to be handed over to their irregular comrades.

With fists clenched, the eight-man crew of an artillery piece of the Communist New Fourth Army pose. The gun is a captured Japanese Type 41 75mm mountain gun which would have been a rare weapon in the Communist arsenal. It was a particularly useful gun for a guerrilla army as it could be easily broken down into six sections and transported on mules or ponies.

A trio of Communist machine-gunners pose for this propaganda photograph with their captured Japanese Type 3 heavy machine guns. Here two of the guerrillas give the cameraman the 'thumbs up', while the other has lost his arm during the war. The Communists depended on their enemies including puppet troops to supply most of their weaponry. Puppet troops even loaned their machine guns to the Communists as long as they were returned whenever the Japanese inspected their units!

Japanese cavalry charge across a Chinese river at full gallop with their Model 44 cavalry carbines slung over their backs in 1943. The Imperial army's cavalry units came into their own in the fighting in China and played an important role in most anti-guerrilla operations. All these troopers are wearing winter coats and have extra ammunition in the canvas ammunition pouches worn around their waists.

Japanese youth volunteers who have been sent to China to bolster the weakened Japanese garrisons after 1941 are spending a day working in the field. As more and more front-line troops were moved to the Pacific and Burmese theatres, 'patriotic' volunteers like these were sent to replace them. As they often came under attack while away from the relative safety of their garrison, these young men were usually armed.

A Japanese mobile workshop in northern China repairs Type 94 tankettes in the field, while a sentry guards the workmen. As less equipment and weaponry was sent to China after 1941, it was essential to ensure the existing tanks, trucks and other vehicles were well maintained. The Japanese Imperial army's second line units were increasingly in danger of guerrilla attack in China during the early 1940s and the guard must be on the alert.

A column of marching Communist guerrillas move through a village to show their strength to the people. The fact that no firearms are visible amongst this group points to the severe shortage of rifles in the Communist ranks. Nearly all the firearms used by the Communists were captured from the Japanese or the Nationalists. Under the terms of the United Front signed in 1937 the Nationalist government of Chiang Kai-shek was supposed to supply them with weapons. Not surprisingly, few rifles or machine guns were supplied, except in the form of captures from the Nationalists.

Hiding behind a tree, Communist guerrillas prepare to pull the chord to ignite a 'string-pull mine' aimed at a passing Japanese patrol in 1945. Communist irregulars supported their regular comrades in the New 4th and 8th Group Armies from 1937–45. As the regular Communist forces expanded these men were easily absorbed into their ranks as a ready trained reserve. Rifles were always in short supply with the guerrillas and homemade booby traps had to be used in their place.

Well-armed Chinese Nationalist guerrillas on parade at their base in late September 1942. These men belong to a so-called 'Revenge Detachment', raised from civilians whose families had suffered under Japanese occupation. The older man near the centre of the group is the leader and is armed with a old C-96 automatic pistol. According to the original caption to the photograph, the whole of his family was killed by the Japanese and this led him to form this resistance group.

This Czechoslovakian Communist postcard was published after the Second World War in celebration of the Chinese Communist army and guerrillas during the conflict. It shows the meeting between regulars of the Communist New Fourth Army and their guerrilla comrades. The Communists relied on the large irregular force to replace casualties in the regular New 4th and 8th Group armies. Although romanticized in this image, the unity of the Communist forces was to lead to their victory in the post-war civil war with the Nationalists in 1949.

Chapter Seven

The Chinese Army in Burma, 1942-5

When the Japanese Imperial navy's aircraft attacked the US Pacific Fleet at Pearl Harbor on 7 December 1941 China's war changed. Overnight the Chinese had Allies against Japan who Chiang Kai-shek hoped would aid him in his four-year war. However, the reality was different with the Japanese blitzkrieg tearing through British, US and Dutch territories by early 1942. In the short term the Allies had enough to cope with without sending armaments or any other aid to Nationalist China. French Indo-China had already been taken over by the Japanese in 1940, cutting off supplies to the Nationalists from that direction. When the Japanese Imperial army invaded British Burma from Thailand on 15 December the last land supply line along the Burma Road was threatened. As with Malaya, the Philippines and other Allied territories, the Japanese advanced through Burma. They moved northwards with the British forces retreating in front of them towards the Burma Road in the north-east of the territory.

By March 1942 Chiang had realized that as the fighting continued in northern Burma unless he offered forces to help the British they would soon be defeated. A Chinese expeditionary force, under the command of US General Stilwell, was deployed to north-eastern Burma. The Chinese sent some of their best troops into Burma, consisting of three armies, each with three divisions (Fifth Army: 22nd, 96th and 200th divisions; Sixty-sixth Army: 28th, 29th and 38th divisions; and Sixth Army: 49th, 55th and 93rd divisions). The 200th Division included eighty Soviet-supplied T-26 light tanks. Although this force appeared formidable on paper, each army was only the strength of a British or US division. Over the next two months the expeditionary corps fought well in several battles with the Japanese, especially their superior divisions such as the 22nd and 38th. By late May the British and their Chinese allies were defeated and began a long retreat into India in the north-west and into Yunnan province in China.

Once the British army defeated in Burma had reorganized itself in the relative safety of India, it was decided that the Allies would train and equip a Chinese army.

This force would be created from the Nationalist troops who had escaped Burma with the elite 22nd and 38th divisions forming a hardcore. It was agreed that the Allies would provide training, equipment and weaponry for a large number of troops, to be designated 'X', or X-Ray, Force. A large training facility made up of various training schools was opened in 1942, with facilities to instruct trainees in military skills such as radio operation, veterinary care for draught animals and artillery operation. With good-quality food, new uniforms, equipment and weapons and proper medical care the Allies were confident they could produce a useful military force. In November 1942 Chiang Kai-shek promised twenty divisions' worth of troops, which would be flown by Allied transport planes across the Himalayas. Training went well and by 1943 a 50,000-strong X Force with modern small arms, artillery and a tank force was ready to be sent into Burma.

From 1943 onwards, two other forces were trained in China by US advisors, with the first, known as 'Y', or Yoke, Force, set up in Yunnan province. The training for Y Force was not as intensive as that given to X Force in India but the troops and officers trained in Yunnan were still superior to most other Nationalist formations. By the early summer of 1943 a force of 100,000 Nationalist troops was available to be sent into Burma. Y Force was designated to advance westwards into Burma along the Salween River to link up with X Force advancing eastwards from India in 1944. A third smaller force, known as 'Z', or Zebra, Force was trained in Kwangsi province from late 1943. The intention was to create a thirty-division-strong force which would be given several roles in any 1944 campaign. With over 2,000 US instructors but with less facilities and few arms to hand to their trainees, Z Force would not reach the standard of either X or Y Forces. Z Force's first role was to advance southwards to link up with any future Allied amphibious landing in southern China. Its other role was to provide a defence force for the US airbases being set up in Nationalist territory from where bombing missions would be launched against Japan.

By December 1943 X Force was ready to begin its advance but the planned link-up with Y Force was to be frustrated by Chiang Kai-shek. Chiang wanted to keep the newly trained troops in Yunnan to counter the threat of rebellious generals, particularly the province's governor, General Lung Yun. Eventually, after threats by the Allies to withdraw their support, Y Force was sent across the Salween River into Burma in May 1944. Both forces had to fight not only against the Japanese Imperial army but in some of the most challenging terrain in the world. It took X Force until March 1944 to reach their first objective, the town of Maingkwan. When it fell Chinese labourers immediately moved in to start repairs on the vital Burma Road. Meanwhile, X Force continued its slow advance, taking Myitkyina in May and Bhamo in November. By January 1945 X Force was in a position to finally link up with Y Force, which it duly did on the 21st. It had taken Y Force until September 1944 to capture their first major town, Tengchung, after an epic battle. After the reopening of the Burma Road, Y Force had served its purpose and most of its units were sent back into China to defend several provinces under attack by the Japanese. X Force, the best of all the Allied trained Nationalist armies, was to be airlifted into northern China and its divisions were to be destroyed in the civil war in Manchuria in 1948.

Soldiers of the Chinese Expeditionary Force that fought in Burma during the doomed British defence of their territory in 1942 hastily dig tank traps. The nine Nationalist divisions sent to aid the British empire forces included the 200th Mechanized Division. The 200th had a large number of Soviet-supplied T-26 light tanks and was the only large Chinese armoured unit. Although the performance of the Chinese in Burma was mixed, some units did put up a good fight against the advancing Japanese Imperial army.

Two machine-gunners of the Chinese Expeditionary Force in Burma prepare to fire their Danish Madsen M1930 machine gun in 1942. The Nationalist formations sent to help the desperate British army in Burma in May 1942 were amongst the best available and were sent by Chiang Kai-shek under protest. He knew, however, that if the British were defeated then all military aid across the Burmese border into western China would be cut off by the Japanese.

A Nationalist soldier of the Chinese Expeditionary Force runs through the jungle in the Toungoo Sector of the fighting. The 5th and 6th armies that made up the force put up a good fight against the invading Japanese on several occasions during the 1942 campaign. This camouflaged soldier has fixed his bayonet to his Mauser rifle which makes it rather cumbersome in the thick jungle. Desperate Allied commanders in Burma were reluctant at first to accept the help of the Chinese, whose fighting capability they had a poor opinion of. Some Nationalist units were to prove them wrong and were to enhance the reputation of Chinese soldiery amongst the British command.

Confident Japanese troops advance into Burma in 1942 as the Imperial army and navy begins its conquest of South-East Asia. The Sino-Japanese War had been underway for almost four years when the Japanese launched their blitzkrieg in Asia. These soldiers could soon face their old enemies, the Chinese, fighting in support of the British empire forces defending Burma. Most of the machine-gunners are carrying ZB-26 light machine guns captured from the Chinese in earlier fighting.

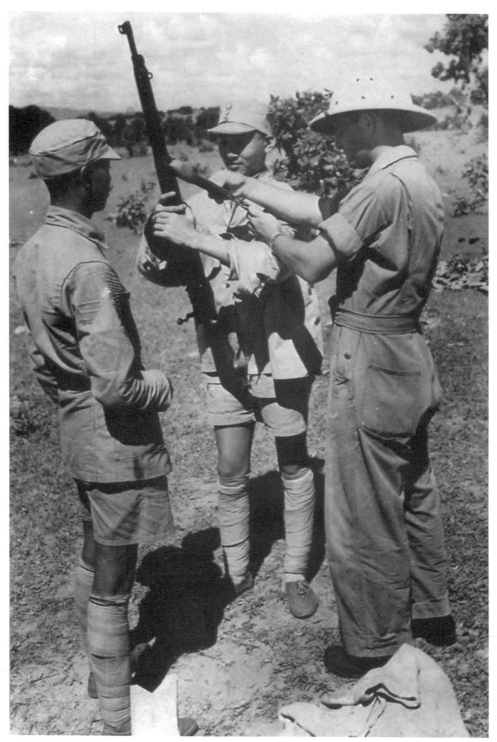

A Nationalist recruit receives small arms training with a P-17 rifle from a US army instructor, who in turn is teaching the Chinese officer to give tuition to other recruits. The US instructors gave thousands of Chinese soldiers training in small arms, artillery and other military skills. Many complimented their Nationalist pupils on their positive attitude and their aptitude in learning these new skills.

Nationalist survivors of the 1942 fighting in Burma take part in an assault course as part of their training in India. The helmets worn by the troops are M35s brought back from Burma by them, while their P-17 rifles have been donated by the Allies. With good training, regular meals and better uniforms, equipment and weaponry these soldiers soon became the elite of the Nationalist army.

A US army instructor looks on as the crew of a PACK 75mm howitzer supplied by the USA fires its gun in the hills around the Ramgarh training centre in September 1943. US instructors were sent to set up a training scheme for the Nationalist artillery which involved new trainees then going on to instruct their comrades. The week-long training course was in most cases found to be adequate to get the Chinese up to a reasonable standard.

A Chinese Nationalist general visits troops from X Force training at one of the Indian training camps at Ramgarh. The general peers down the sights of the US-supplied medium mortar while his entourage of US and Nationalist officers look on. Allied plans were for the Chinese Nationalist divisions trained in India to take the war in Burma to the Japanese. Meanwhile, Chiang Kai-shek saw the well-trained and well-armed divisions of Nationalist troops as a future elite for his army to replace his best units destroyed in 1937–8.

Soldiers of Y Force, the Allied trained and supplied army based in Yunnan province, cross a river in June 1943. Y Force was made up of eleven infantry divisions which were intended to enter Burma sometime in 1943–4. Their arms, equipment and training were not up to the standard of their sister organization, X Force, in India but were superior to other Nationalist formations. They were to be pitted against the 56th Division of the Japanese Imperial army fighting in some the most difficult terrain encountered during the Second World War.

A young Nationalist soldier of Y Force poses near his outpost showing the camouflage used to protect against Japanese air attack. He is wearing the basic khaki drill shirt, shorts and field cap issued by the Allies to their trainee soldiers in Yunnan province. His two stick-type grenades are either leftovers from those imported from Germany in the 1930s or more like locally produced copies of them. The canvas grenade carrier worn by this young soldier has again been produced in local Chinese workshops.

A Nationalist sentry relaxes at his post with a clever improvisation to shade him from the searing heat. The young soldier is part of the Chinese force stationed along the Salween River from 1943–4. Sickness was a major killer of Chinese and Japanese troops who faced each other across the Salween Gorge in western China. Malaria was endemic to this region, which was in fact listed amongst the worst areas in the world for this particular disease in the 1940s.

Wounded Nationalist troops of Y Force are taken back to the rear by stretcher bearers, while the walking wounded are supported by their comrades in 1943. The long-suffering Chinese soldier would often receive little in the way of medical treatment and a minor wound was often fatal. A shortage of doctors and medical facilities and the long journey from the front line to the nearest field hospital raised the mortality rate far beyond the level in other Allied armies.

A Japanese detachment are inspected before moving up to their positions on the Salween River Front in 1943. Japanese units facing the Nationalists across the Salween River had chased the Chinese north-eastwards out of Burma in 1942. Most of the Imperial troops on the Salween Front were hardened veterans of the fighting in the Philippines, the Dutch East Indies. These soldiers are armed with the usual Arisaka Type 38 rifles and Type 11 light machine guns. The kind of terrain that they will be operating in is evidenced by the tree saw carried by the soldier in the foreground.

This photograph sums up the state of most of the Nationalist army as mules pull their howitzer along the Burma Road in 1944. The gun and limber are piled high with the kit and personal belongings of its crew, including clanking metal cooking pots. The gun is a Soviet-supplied 4.5in MK I howitzer which had originally belonged to the British army. After being sold to the Imperial Russian army in the First World War, it entered service with the Red Army after 1917. Others had been supplied to the White Russian Army between 1918 and 1922 and then captured by the Soviet Union after their defeat.

A US soldier from Merrill's Marauders lights the cigarette of his wounded Nationalist Chinese ally. US and British troops who fought alongside Chinese troops were often impressed and frustrated at the same time by their Allies. They were in awe of the Chinese soldiers' bravery and hardiness but were less impressed by their tactics. Nationalist troops, for instance, would gain a position and then halt or refuse to advance if this meant putting 'precious' equipment and weaponry at risk of capture.

Lieutenant General Joseph W. Stilwell, the senior US representative in China from 1942 to 1944, with Nationalist General Sun Li-jen in 1944. Sun Li-jen was the highly regarded commanding officer of the 'elite' 38th Division which fought in Burma in 1942. He was one of the few Nationalist generals that managed to gain Stilwell's grudging respect. Overall Stilwell had a poor opinion of the Chinese leadership, whether military or civil, and was particularly scathing of Chiang Kai-shek. Stilwell's strained relationship with Chiang led to his recall to the USA in late 1944 and his replacement by a more 'amiable' representative.

A machine-gunner of the Allied trained X Force runs along a jungle path with the tripod for his US M1917 heavy machine gun over his shoulder. The M1917 water cooled machine gun was the main type issued by the Allied powers to their Nationalist Chinese allies. Unlike the majority of the Nationalist army in China, X Force troops were issued with just a few models of small arms. With standard small arms, a reliable supply of ammunition for them and good rations the Nationalist troops trained in India performed well in action.

Nationalist Artillerymen of the Allied trained X Force haul their 75mm PACK howitzer up a slope along a jungle path in Burma. The PACK howitzer was the most common type of artillery piece in service with X Force and was ideal for the terrain that they would soon be fighting in. Although units were later issued with mules to haul the artillery, this gun is relying on sheer manpower to get it into position. All the crewmen have been issued with British khaki drill shirts and shorts and US M2 steel helmets.

A couple of Nationalist soldiers meet in Burma in 1944. The man on the left belongs to X Force. His comrade is from one of the Nationalist formations trained and armed by the Allies in Yunnan province, Y Force. It is noticeable that the X Force soldier has been given a smart Allied uniform, including a US M2 steel helmet. He has been issued with a Thompson sub-machine gun from Allied stocks, while the other man still uses a Mauser rifle. The Y Force soldier has a rather scruffier uniform and unlike his comrade has straw sandals instead of leather boots.

Soldiers of the Allied trained X Force advance into Burma with one man's pet monkey taking a ride on his backpack. Generally, the Nationalist soldiers of X Force had high morale as they were better fed and equipped than the rest of the Chinese army. During their training in India these soldiers went on long route marches to prepare them for their role in Burma. Veterans of the X Force divisions went on to form the elite of the post-1945 Nationalist army before being destroyed in the Chinese civil war of 1946–9.

This poster was issued by the US government in 1944 to promote the co-operation between the Chinese army in Burma and the Allies. At the bottom of the poster the Chinese characters read 'Brothers in Arms to Defeat Japanese Bandits'. The relationship between the Chinese Nationalist troops and their US and British Allies was not always an easy one. Different attitudes about the way that a modern war should be fought often created frustrations on each side.

A couple of young Nationalist soldiers of X Force patrol along a Burmese river bank armed with US-supplied Thompson sub-machine guns in 1945. They are wearing the usual mixture of British and US uniforms with India pattern jumpers and US fatigue caps.

A Stuart M3A3 light tank of the Provisional Tank Group of the Chinese Nationalist army in Burma moves quickly down a jungle track. The majority of tanks in use with this US-trained armoured formation were this so-called light model. In reality, it was more than a match for any Japanese Imperial army tank it might encounter on the Burmese Front in 1944–5.

Sherman M4/A4 medium tanks of the Provisional Tank Group of the Nationalist army's X Force in Burma move down a road. The tank at the front has been decorated with what appears to be a cat's face with its whiskers radiating out of the barrel. All the crew have been issued with US tank overalls and leather crash helmets by their US training personnel. Most Chinese tank drivers had never even driven a car before joining the tank unit but were reported to have soon mastered the skill. As one US instructor remarked, the only thing most of the men had driven was a 'bullock cart on their farms'.

Chapter Eight

China's Final Victory, 1943-5

By 1943 the Sino-Japanese War had been fought for six long years and both the Japanese and the Chinese were exhausted. War weariness amongst the Japanese in China had become a major problem with no end to the war in sight. The ever expected Nationalist collapse had never materialized and all Japan's efforts to subdue the Chinese had failed. Some Chinese had collaborated with the Japanese but they were despised by the vast majority of the population. The Japanese population's enthusiasm for the war had also faded as more and more of their sons' ashes were returned home for burial. However, the Japanese were still committed to their occupation of China and over 1,000,000 men were still serving there. With no hope of further reinforcements for China, especially in terms of weapons and equipment, the Japanese Imperial army could not defeat the Chinese. The Japanese were unable to defeat Nationalist China before they had commitments to their Pacific War, from December 1941. Now with Allied aid supporting China, even if in limited quantities, the Chinese were getting stronger as the Japanese were weakening. A stalemate now existed in China and the Japanese Imperial army no longer had the will to try and defeat the Chinese. At the same time, the Nationalist and Communist forces could not hope in the short term to defeat such large Japanese forces stationed in China. Japanese tactics had also changed since 1941 with the emphasis now on holding onto what they had gained rather than trying to conquer more territory. When they went out on operations the main aim of the Japanese was to take food and other supplies from the population. As time went on, the Japanese Imperial army was less willing to confront Chinese forces, whether regular or guerrilla. At the same time, the average Chinese soldier had lost their inferiority complex towards the Japanese army and its soldiers.

Although the Chinese theatre was still important to the Japanese, the situation with the Allies was to take on more significance. Their struggles in the Pacific from 1942–5 and with the British in Burma from 1943–5 became more important. Much of their heavy equipment had, however, been transported to other theatres and in particular the Pacific

Islands. Because of their weaknesses the Japanese Imperial army had now to concentrate on trying to control the guerrilla threat in China until 1945 (see Chapter 6).

In one final desperate effort to reverse their decline in China the Imperial army launched a large-scale offensive. In April 1944, the 'Ichi-Go', or 'Number One', offensive was begun and was to be one of Japan's last major operations in China. Huge Japanese forces were marshalled for the offensive with 400,000 men, 1,500 artillery pieces and 800 tanks taken from all over China. Ichi-Go was divided into two separate operations with the first, 'Ka-Go', aimed at destroying all Nationalist forces still north of the Yangtze River. One of Ka-Go's aims was to surround and destroy the Nationalist army that held part of the Peking–Wuhan railway. This objective was easily achieved, although the Japanese advance was limited by lack of supplies once they out reached their supply lines. A second phase, known as Operation 'U-Go', was to be launched once Ka-Go had got underway. The aim of U-Go was to knock out the airbases of the US 14th Air Force which were being used to bomb the Japanese mainland. After destroying these airbases the combined Japanese force was to advance into Szechwan province with the ultimate aim of capturing the wartime capital Chungking. Nationalist divisions facing the offensive were made up of poorly trained and armed conscripts who were soon demoralized and fell back in front of the advancing Japanese. U-Go was a great success and the US air bases fell in quick succession as the Nationalist forces retreated in confusion. On 8 August the city of Hengyang, to the east of the Chinese capital, fell to the Japanese and it seemed that an advance on Chungking was now inevitable. As the campaign in southern China dragged into November 1944, however, the Japanese began to run out of food and other supplies. Vital air cover was also lost when the Japanese had to send its fighters to Japan to defend their homeland. Over the next few months Ichi-Go ground to a halt and the Chinese finally began to make some successful counter-attacks. Chiang Kai-shek had been proved right when he said that 'The Japanese will run out of blood before the Chinese will run out of ground'.

In April and May 1945 the Japanese launched what was to be their last offensive in China with the aim of capturing a US air base at Chihchiang. The Chihchiang Offensive was launched from territory recently taken during the Ichi-Go operation. Large Nationalist forces were stationed to halt the advance and after being reinforced to a strength of four divisions they threw back the Japanese. In early 1945 the Japanese Imperial High Command had already introduced plans to consolidate their positions in China. By withdrawing units from outlying garrisons in southern China they intended to concentrate them in central China in the region of Wuhan. Other formations would be gathered in the Canton region and in the Peking region, where they faced less opposition from guerrilla forces. As the Japanese tried to move their forces into these fastnesses they came under attack by Chinese guerrillas. In August a new threat had to be faced in Manchuria, which although not strictly involved in the Sino-Japanese War, was to influence its end greatly. The Soviet Union's victory in Europe in April 1945 released huge numbers of troops to take part in a new offensive in Manchuria. Since the 1900s Japan had always feared an attack in the East by the Red Army but a neutrality pact signed between the Soviet Union and Japan in the 1930s had held. Now that Japan was on the verge of defeat, the Soviet Union decided to renege on this agreement and on 8 August they struck. With an overwhelming army of 1,500,000 men, 26,000 artillery pieces, 3,700 tanks and 500 combat aircraft, they launched a blitzkrieg offensive that swept the Kwangtung Army away. The Kwangtung Army was a substantial size on paper but out-of-date tanks, obsolete artillery and depleted units were the reality. Soviet claims of 84,000 Japanese dead and almost 600,000 prisoners taken were not disputed. Although not really part of the Sino-Japanese War, this was a devastating defeat for the Imperial army in East Asia.

However, the end in China was be dictated by events elsewhere and with Japan's defeat in the Pacific and the dropping of atomic bombs in August 1945, the war was over. On 2 September all Japanese military forces in China officially surrendered to the victorious Chinese, both Nationalist and Communist. Most Japanese military and civilian personnel were repatriated quickly with a surprising lack of violence from the triumphant Chinese. Nationalist China's victory was to prove illusionary as within a short time conflict was to break out with the Communists. After a brief interlude and attempts at mediation between Chiang Kai-shek and Mao Tse-tung, the civil war between the Chinese Nationalists and Communists was to resume in 1946.

Nationalist troops are moved up the Yangtze River in a flotilla of river junks during a Chinese offensive in 1943. Although the cliffs rising up from the river will provide some cover for troops on the move, they will still be vulnerable to Japanese air attack. After the disaster of the 1940 Nationalist offensives and with more precious equipment and manpower lost, any further operations had to limited ones. This did not stop the Chinese from launching small-scale attacks on the Japanese whenever they saw a weakness in their enemy.

During a Japanese offensive an infantry section moves across a street under fire while a shell from its artillery bursts in the distance in 1943. The Imperial army's offensives by this stage in the war were usually aimed at specific objectives rather than capturing more territory. One of the main battles in this year was for the city of Changteh, which was fought over for a month-and-a-half in November and December. Many Japanese soldiers of the post-1941 period were not up to the standard of the first troops who had fought in China in 1937–41.

On the banks of the Yangtze River in May 1943 Nationalist troops wait patiently to board civilian junks to be moved to the front. Some of the troops are wearing bamboo versions of the M35 steel helmet which may from a distance look like the real thing. Obviously, this headgear would provide no protection for the soldier but at this stage of the war nothing else was available. Uniforms and equipment used by much of the Chinese army after 1941 had to made using local resources. Although the Allies were providing arms to the forces trained in India and western China, the majority of the army used rifles imported before 1939.

A Nationalist army machine-gunner aims his ZB-26 light machine gun from behind a wall reduced to rubble during the battle for Changteh in December 1943. He belongs to the 57th Division which fought bitterly with the Japanese for control of the city, with only a few hundred surviving the battle.

Captured Japanese soldiers are brought into Nationalist headquarters at Changteh during the battle for the city in 1943. The handful of troops captured in the battle were photographed by Western journalists as few Imperial army soldiers made the decision to surrender. As the war progressed, the Communists even had a few units fighting for them made up of turncoats and pro-Communist Japanese. Of course, any ex-Imperial army soldiers captured by their former comrades would have received little mercy.

Nationalist Major General Feng Yuan, the commander of 11th Division, plans his next move during fighting for the city of Changteh in November 1943. The city was attacked by a Japanese force of 100,000 but the Chinese garrison held out and fought the attacking Japanese back in bitter street fighting. Although the city fell to the Imperial army on 3 December, it had been recaptured by the Chinese by the 9th, forcing the Japanese to withdraw.

Exhausted Japanese troops take a well-needed break during an anti-guerrilla operation in 1944. By this time the Imperial army had been fighting in China for seven years and war weariness had become a major problem. With large numbers of Japanese soldiers being transferred to the Pacific Theatre the Imperial army could not hope to defeat the Chinese. Many of the replacements sent to China from 1941 onwards were not up to the standard of the veterans.

Japanese Imperial army troops advance from their defensive position during an offensive in central China in 1944. By this stage in the war the Japanese had given up any thoughts of further territorial conquest in China and most offensives were launched simply to disrupt the Chinese war effort. Imperial army resources were being weakened as more and more troops were switched to the Pacific Theatre. This machine-gun unit is supporting a Type 94 light tank which although obsolete in all other theatres, was still being used by the Imperial army in China until 1945.

Japanese youth volunteers, making up part of the garrison at an Imperial army outpost in occupied China, march out on patrol. Isolated Japanese fortresses like this were often easy prey for the Communist guerrillas in the latter stages of the Sino-Japanese War. Both the sentry taking the salute and some of the young volunteers are armed with 'war booty' Mauser rifles captured from the Nationalist army.

With most sources of imported small arms cut off by 1940 the Nationalist army had to rely on its own resources. This underground armoury is producing copies of the Czech ZB-26 light machine gun while repairing others. There had always been a large number of armouries throughout China since the 1800s but their total output could never meet demand. By 1944, when this photograph was taken, some small arms were being supplied to the Chinese by the Allies. Most of these went to the troops being trained in India and western China for service in Burma.

Fighting in the ruins of the city of Teng-Chung in western Yunnan province, a Nationalist machine-gun crew fire towards Japanese positions in 1944. The machine gun is a ZB-53, sold by Czechoslovakia to Chinese in the 1930s and used in large numbers throughout the war. By this time some veterans of the Nationalist army had been fighting for seven years and had largely overcome their inferiority complex when facing their Japanese enemy. One of the crewmen has a shovel stuck in his backpack to dig in his machine gun during the heavy street fighting for the city.

Smiling Chinese Nationalist troops and their US advisor show off war booty taken from the Japanese in the fighting for Teng-Chung in September 1944. The haul includes two Japanese war flags and a few steel helmets and what appear to be a couple of Type 3 tank machine guns taken from an Imperial army light tank. An ex-Chinese MP-28 sub-machine gun, captured by the Japanese and then re-captured by the Nationalists, is held by the soldier in the middle foreground.

A US ground crewman and a Nationalist soldier defend a US airbase from Japanese air attack in early 1945. The B-29 Super Fortress bases in south-eastern China allowed the US air force to bomb Japanese cities and for this reason were a target of the 1944–5 Imperial army offensives. Interestingly, the rifle used by the Chinese soldier is a Japanese Arisaka Type 38, while his ally fires a Browning M1919 A4 machine gun.

A Nationalist 75mm PACK howitzer belonging to the Second Army is firing from a dug-in position in southern China in spring 1944. Most of these US-supplied guns were given to the forces trained in India and fighting on the Burma Front in 1944–5. This 75mm is on the older type of carriage with metal wheels instead of the newer version with tyres.

The Nationalist crew of a US-supplied M1 81mm mortar fires towards advancing Japanese divisions taking part in the Ichi-Go offensive. They are part of a force defending the large US airbase at Chihchiang to the south-west of the Nationalist capital at Chungking. One of Japan's aims with the 1944–5 offensive was to destroy any airbases from where B-29 bombers were being launched against Japan.

Soviet-supplied T-26 light tanks rumble past a reviewing stand at a military parade in Yunnan province in 1944. These tanks are some of the survivors from the Nationalist 200th Mechanized Division which fought in Burma in 1942. Yunnan province, in western China, was one of the few regions of the country that was relatively safe from Japanese attack. It was under the control of the powerful General Lung Yun, who had remained largely independent of Chiang Kai-shek's control since 1927.

Communist troops examine captured telephone wire and rails brought into their base by guerrillas in summer 1945. The Communists were almost completely blockaded by the Nationalist divisions during the 1941–5 period. With few military and other supplies getting into the blockaded area, the Communists had constantly to improvise. Telephone wire was used to extend their underground communication system, while rails were made into arms and ammunition in their workshops.

This nice image of a young Communist cavalryman in 1945 shows an elite soldier of the Chinese Red Army. The Communists made great use of their cavalry arm during the Sino-Japanese War, especially in the latter years of the conflict. This soldier's relatively smart uniform, equipment and modern Mauser 98k rifle indicate that he belongs to one of the better cavalry units. However, the lack of clips for his rifle in the canvas bandolier over his shoulder is evidence of the shortage of ammunition suffered by the Communists.

These Nationalist troops are undergoing specialist training at a US-run commando training school in May 1945. The school ran courses in irregular warfare and also a paratroopers' course with selected Nationalist volunteers. US instructors came from the Office of Strategic Services, the forerunner of the Central Intelligence Agency, and several training camps were set up in western China. Uniforms, weaponry and equipment are of US origin with P-17 rifles and Thompson sub-machine guns.

Nationalist soldiers listen to a motivational speech by their commanding officer in spring 1945. The soldiers belong to a newly organized division raised in Free China and armed and equipped from the Nationalist government's resources. Uniforms worn by the men are locally made, as are the sandals, which may have been made by the soldiers themselves. The field caps were also manufactured in local workshops and have a cloth badge featuring a white sun on a blue sky sewn on the front. Their Mauser rifles are the short model sold to China by Czechoslovakia and Belgium in the mid- to late 1930s.

A Nationalist sentry stands guard at a roadblock at the entrance to Kunming, the capital of Yunnan province in summer 1945. It was here that the Burma Road joined the highway to the Nationalist wartime capital of Chungking. After the reopening of the Burma Road, the first convoy to Kunming reached the city on 1 February 1945. Much of the work to repair the road had been done by thousands of Chinese civilian workers labouring in terrible conditions.

Nationalist troops march through the streets of the south-western Chinese city of Kweilin in August 1944. The civilian population of the city had been largely evacuated as the Japanese Imperial army closed in. As far as can be seen in this image, none of the troops in this long column are armed.

Japanese Imperial army recruits perform a defiant banzai in the closing months of the war in China in 1945. The youth of the soldiers is noticeable and these teenage boys were sent in large numbers to fill the ranks of the depleted Kwangtung Army. Shortages of heavy weaponry was a problem for the Japanese army as tanks and artillery were shipped to Manchuria and the Pacific Islands.

The surrender of all Japanese Imperial army, naval and air force personnel in China took place on 9 September 1945. Japan was represented by General Neiji Okamura and the Nationalist government by General Ho Ying-chin. With high symbolism, the ceremony took place at the Central Military Academy in Nanking. In total, approximately 2 million military and civilian Japanese in China were to be eventually repatriated back to Japan.

Nationalist officers examine a stack of captured Japanese rifles which were part of the huge numbers of armaments surrendered to the Chinese in August 1945. Many of these rifles would find themselves in the hands of the Nationalist troops in the coming civil war with the Communists. The Communists also captured large numbers of Japanese weapons, while others were handed over to them by the Soviet army which had taken them in Manchuria in their August 1945 offensive.

Japanese troops have their kit checked before boarding ships in a northern Chinese port to be repatriated in October 1945. After the bitterness of the Sino-Japanese War the majority of Japanese soldiers and civilians were allowed to return to Japan in an orderly manner. Some Imperial army soldiers were forced to stay in China and help the Communists to train new recruits. Others freely volunteered to fight for the Communists and the Nationalists during the 1946–9 civil war.

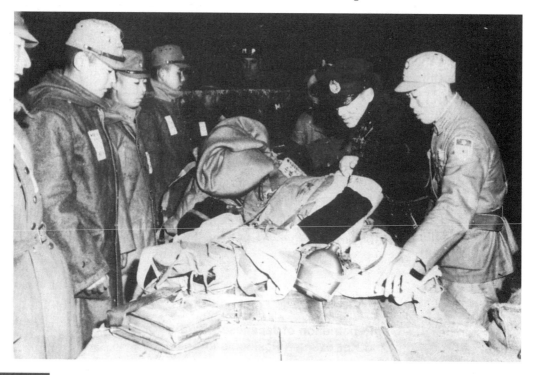